NATURAL RELIGION

Second Edition

NATURAL RELIGION

Re-Connecting
to the Real World

Second Edition

Neal Ferris

Natural Religion by Neal Ferris
Second edition © 2020

Color drawing of ring-tailed mongoose from Madagascar on cover by Cary Grey, a biological illustrator who lived in the seacoast area of New Hampshire. She works in colored pencil, graphite and carbon dust. Her drawings in the text are of a dragonfly, rockweed f. spiralis (seaweed), an opened Tridacna maxima (clam) and a giant sequoia seedling.

Author photo by Sylvia Foster, 2000.

On the quotation of material from this book: Any properly footnoted quotation of up to 200 sequential words may be used without permission as long as the total number of words quoted does not exceed 1000. For longer quotations or for a greater number of total words, please contact the author for permission at naturalreligion@gmail.com

Library of Congress Cataloging-in-Publication Data
Ferris, Neal, 1935-
Natural Religion: Re-connecting to the Real World, by Neal Ferris
ISBN: 978-1-950381-30-2
1. Religion. 2. Philosophy. 3. Science. 4. Psychology. 5. Ecology.

The author is grateful to the following authors and publishers for permission to quote from their works: Brenda J. Dunne, permission to quote from Robert G. Jahn and Brenda J. Dunne, *Margins of Reality*. Orlando, FL: Harcourt Brace & Co. 1987. Wade Davis, his article, "Saving the ethnosphere," *Boston Globe*, 4/28/2002. Stuart Kauffman, *At Home in the Universe*. NY: Oxford University Press. 1995. Rupert Sheldrake, *The Rebirth of Nature*. NY: Bantam Books. 1991. Malidoma Patrice Somé, *The Healing Wisdom of Africa*, Tarcher, Penguin Group (USA). 1988.

To order additional copies of this book, contact:
Piscataqua Press
32 Daniel Street
Portsmouth, NH 03801

This book is intended for people who have no religious persuasion or who are questioning or have rejected their traditional religions and are searching for a point of view that is both spiritual and compatible with science as well as with their own experience. The book deals with issues of human separation from nature and ways in which we may get re-connected with the real world and with ourselves in a time of climate crises.

Many people are searching for a philosophy that "ties it all together" in a manner that is both reasonable and heartening. This book offers a unique way of putting together the pieces of such a world view into a coherent whole and offers helpful suggestions for putting the resulting philosophy into practice.

CONTENTS

Preface to the First Edition   1
   "Take us back to reality."
Preface to Second Edition   4
Introduction   5
   The Wound.

PART I
THE SEVERED CENTER

Chapter One   11
   The Myth
Chapter Two   15
   The Perversion
Chapter Three   19
   The Doctrine
Chapter Four   23
   Omnipotence and Predestination
Chapter Five   27
   The Error of Humanism
Chapter Six   31
   Can Religion Be Natural?

PART II

SEPARATION AND CONNECTION IN RELIGIONS

Chapter One   37
   Animistic Religions
   When God Was A Woman
   African Rhythm
   Native American Religion
   Shinto: The Binding Relationship

Chapter Two   59
   Eastern Religions
   Hinduism: Enough To Make One Wonder
   Buddhism: The Power of Negative Thinking
   Taoism and Confucianism: Nature and Society

Chapter Three   75
   Middle Eastern Religions
   A Book of Many Religions
   Pharisaic Judaism
   Essene Judaism
   Trinitarian Christianity .
   Gnostic Christianity
   Zoroaster, Angels and Essene Christianity
   Islam's Way of Submission

PART III

HUMAN NATURE

Chapter One   123
    The Problem of Objectification
Chapter Two   127
    Feeling Is First
Chapter Three   131
    What Is a Self?
Chapter Four   137
    Is Mind More Than What Brains Do?
Chapter Five   151
    Religion and Sexuality
Chapter Six   157
    The Promise of Human Nature

PART IV

GOD IN NATURE

Chapter One — 171
Cosmology and Creativity

Chapter Two — 181
Creative Evolution

Chapter Three — 193
Emotion Everywhere In a Conscious Cosmos

Chapter Four — 201
A Field for Emotion and Thought

Chapter Five — 215
Pondering the Power of God

Chapter Six — 221
The Problem of Evil

Chapter Seven — 233
Our Future As Individuals

PART V

MENDING THE SEVERED CENTER

Chapter One   243
The Foundation of Morality
Chapter Two   251
Respecting Nature
Chapter Three   265
Natural Healing
Chapter Four   275
A World For Worship

Afterword   281

Epilogue   283
    Natural Religion in a Time of Climate Crises

Acknowledgments

I am indebted to the following people who gave of their time to read my manuscript and offer helpful suggestions: Joyce Ferris, Kathleen and Norman Ferris, Jacqueline and Eric Gratz, Cary Grey and Alan Perkins. Although none are responsible for any deficiencies that may remain, this book is certainly much the better for their kind attention.

Cary Grey also contributed the beautiful drawings that adorn the cover and four of the pages of this book. Her artwork is as graceful as her comments on my manuscript were insightful.

Most of all, I thank my wife, Sylvia Foster, for many, many hours of editorial and technical assistance. Her constant encouragement more than matched my occasional discouragement. I gratefully dedicate this work to her.

Preface to the First Edition

"Take us back to reality."

"Science without religion is lame; religion without science is blind." ~*Albert Einstein*

In his *Myths to Live By,* Joseph Campbell asks, "When people talk of going back to nature, do they really know what they are asking for?" This book addresses that question.

Any reader who thinks that a natural religion must be based solely on the physical aspects of nature—that "natural" must mean "atheistic" or "materialistic"—is in for some surprises. As my title and subtitle indicate, I believe "natural" and "real" to be compatible; however, reality encompasses much more than the merely physical as we shall see.

This book elucidates the main message of my sermons over a forty-year period, as it has been enhanced by reading and thinking since my retirement in 2000 from the parish ministry. The message is *loss of connection and the possibility of re-connection with nature–including our own nature–and affirming our place as members of the earth community.*

The word "religion" comes from a Latin term, "religio," meaning "to tie back." My chapters on religions, especially the Judeo-Christian-Muslim versions of monotheism, focus on how, rather than tying us close to nature, they have contributed to our sense of separation from the source of our life. I also highlight positive contributions of each of the religions as they relate to the human connection with the natural world. The rest of the book is devoted to an understanding of how a life-affirming religion may yet retrieve what has been lost.

The book is divided into five parts. The first part focuses on the loss of connection and makes the case for a natural–as opposed to supernatural religion. As indicated, the second part offers germane lessons from world religions. The third explores applicable characteristics of human nature including feeling, consciousness, and sexuality. The fourth supports a "process philosophy" view of God in nature and includes chapters on evolution, life-energy, and the problem of evil. The last part calls for a return to nature, with implications for healing and morality, justice and economics, and worship.

Whenever we are willing to question ideas that have given our lives coherence and meaning, we run the risk of becoming disoriented, even frightened. As Dr. Christiane Northrup has said, the mind creates antibodies against new ideas. To those who may find some of this book disturbing, I want to acknowledge that, like you, I have had difficulty adapting to a viewpoint that was new to me; however, I eventually found that being flexible was well worth the trouble–as I trust will be the case with those who are able to maintain an open and inquiring mind.

I close with a statement by Sarvepalli Radhakrishnan, philosopher-politician, contemp-orary of Gandhi and President of India: "It is the function of religion to reaffirm the intuitive loyalty to life and solidarity of human nature, to lift us out of the illusion of isolation and take us back to reality."[1] I hope this book may be of some aid to the reader in understanding how that task may be accomplished.

[1] From Radhakrishnan's opening statement in The Philosophy of Sarvepalli *Radhakrishnan*, Volume 8 (1952) of *The Library of Living Philosophers*, edited by Paul A. Schilpp. New York: Tudor Publishing Co.

Preface to Second Edition

Seventeen years after my first edition, I have read more and have updated and improved several parts of this book. This includes the Epilogue that I consider most timely as it addresses urgent issues.

Introduction

The Wound

We are all ailing due to an anti-nature attitude that permeates Western religion, philosophy, and culture.

I began my first edition at a time of daily revelations of sexual abuse of children and adolescents by Roman Catholic priests. A crisis atmosphere still pervades that religious organization. What will transpire remains to be seen, but it is heartening to see prominent Catholics calling for fundamental reform. Eugene Cullen Kennedy, a psychology professor and a former priest, goes to the heart of the matter when he characterizes sexual abuse of children as a symptom of an "underlying wound." He suggests, as the mythologist Joseph Campbell did many years ago, that the issue of this underlying wound is beautifully illustrated in the legend of Parsifal, who set out to find and cure the Grail King, who had sustained a wound on his search for the Holy Grail. The Grail seeker symbolized the spirit. He fought with the Black Knight who represented nature. The Grail seeker killed the Black Knight but was wounded by a spear that passed through his genitals. Dr. Kennedy summed up the issue as it has persisted for centuries: ***"In vanquishing Nature, Spirit sustains a wound that will not heal."***

Dr. Kennedy characterized the priest pedophilia crisis

as ". . . but one symptom of the unhealed wound that resulted from the official church's strike at the unity of human personality." That unity is shattered whenever people are divided into two warring factions: soul versus body, spirit versus nature, and when human beings are made to feel guilty about their sexuality. Dr. Kennedy described how the church, ". . . seeking to overpower nature, wounds itself and its people whenever it blindly enters or boldly distorts the most intimate area of their lives."[1]

This "wounded-ness" is by no means confined to the Roman Catholic Church. We are all ailing to one degree or another because of a fundamental human "splitting" that has its roots in ancient history. This severing of our centeredness in nature had a cause. And it can be cured. First, we must be clear about the cause.

In what follows, I show how far back this wound goes in religious and social history: its origins and how it has been kept open and festering in some—but by no means all—Christian teachings. I also show how a fragmented Western philosophy and science have reduced nature to a valueless "thing" to be exploited regardless of the social and ecological consequences.

As an example of such consequence, consider the growing practice of "bio-piracy." The Indian physicist, ecologist and activist, Vandana Shiva, has spoken eloquently concerning some of the disastrous results of our wounded way of thinking and living. Writing of the close relationship between the natural principles of regeneration and sustainability, she notes that ". . . the continuity between regeneration in human and non-human nature that was the basis for all ancient worldviews was broken by patriarchy. People were separated from nature, and the creativity involved in processes of regeneration was denied. Creativity became the monopoly of men . . . The source of patriarchal power over women and nature lies in separation and fragmentation."[2]

The first part of this book is devoted to an understanding of separation and fragmentation. Once that issue is clarified, we may consider the possibility of reconnection: how a natural religion takes us back to reality.

[1] Eugene Cullen Kennedy, "Church's wound stays unhealed." *Boston Globe*, 3/10/02.
[2] Vandana Shiva, *Biopiracy: The Plunder of Nature and Knowledge*. Boston: South End Press, 1997, p. 43f, 63.

PART I

THE SEVERED CENTER

"Man's heart, away from nature, grows cold."
~*Luther Standing Bear (c.1868-1939)*

Chapter One

The Myth

The anti-nature attitude lies at the root of the "creation"-by-severing story in Genesis.

Despite being the most "believed" collection of books in our culture, the Judeo-Christian Bible is still usually misunderstood, and, therefore, misrepresented. It is ironic that conviction of the uniqueness and divine inspiration of the Genesis accounts of the world's origins still predominates in religious circles, despite the fact that, since 1876, several versions of much earlier Babylonian and Assyrian creation epics have been known to biblical scholars. These scholars have noted their influence on the writing of Genesis I, especially the first of the two creation stories (Gen. 1, 2:4a).

Much has been said about the sense of alienation or estrangement that underlies the need for religion (and psychotherapy) in our society, without mention of the crucial role played by the beginning verses of the Bible, the Judeo-Christian-Muslim myth of creation: "When God set out to create Heaven and Earth, He found nothing around Him but Tohu (Hebrew for chaos, desolation) and Bohu (emptiness, void). The face of

Tehom (the deep), over which His Spirit hovered, was clothed in darkness." After speaking light into existence, "He made a firmament to divide the Upper Waters from the Lower Waters . . ." The earth emerged from the Lower Waters that became the sea.[1]

This myth, written down by Hebrew priests about 750 B.C.E., is based on much earlier (roughly 1000 years) Babylonian and Assyrian creation epics, one of which tells of the upstart god, Marduk, who caught the mother-goddess, Tiamat, in his net and split her in two, using the halves to form heaven and earth.

Usually missed in pious readings of Genesis, is the obvious point that the Hebrew God does NOT create "out of nothing." Tohu, Bohu, and Tehom already existed, according to the text. Tehom, a feminine term reminiscent of the Babylonian Tiamat, is conceived as a deep, watery substance, which the Hebrew God (following Marduk) "divides," severing what had been united. This separation is not an act of creation: it is an act of violence that results in the destruction of a previously existing creation and the formation of a new ordering of existence. Tehom, by then an abstraction, was severed by the younger male, warrior-god.

The Biblical myth summarizes the Hebrew suppression of goddess worship that had lasted many thousands of years before the conquest of Palestine. The goddess is characterized in the Old Testament as an "abomination." For example, I Kings 11:5, "For Solomon went after Ashtoreth the goddess of the Sidonians, and after Milcom the abomination of the Ammonites."

Following the lead of mythologist, Joseph Campbell and archaeologist, Marija Gimbutas, present-day feminist scholars and theologians show how the Bible may be read in large part as a documentation of the suppression of the much older goddess-worship by a male-dominated religious culture. In the myths of other traditions, any sense of separation from the divine foundation of our nature is usually explained by a misunderstanding or some fatal coincidence, or simple curiosity. Whatever the cause, the human mind then perceives the world in the light—I should say, the darkness—of this estrangement, a condition of separateness, and, therefore, aloneness. We then mis-perceive the world, because of our fundamental confusion. That sense of alienation has caused people to armor themselves against the world and even to armor themselves against their own nature and to pay a heavy price for so doing—as I trust much of this book will help to clarify.

This "severing," this rejection of the ancient understanding of creation as an organic process of conception and birth and its replacement with a hierarchical re-ordering by the words issuing from the god's brain, is supported by the primary myth of the Bible, the holy book of Jewish, Christian, and Muslim religion. Everything that follows this first Biblical story rests on that mentality.

The Biblical myth tells us about the "wound." It illustrates a world characterized by a fundamental split both within the human mind and between humanity and nature. The wellspring of the feeling for life, the felt connection with nature and the integrity of the human mind itself has been severed; so that, as the second Hebrew myth shows us, instead of living at peace in the Garden of Eden, the man and woman are led to disobey and, as a consequence, be thrust into a state of estrangement—at war with their own nature: mind against body, spirit against flesh, man against woman and both against nature (Gen. 2:4b, Chapter 3).

This double-myth that permeates our culture tells of a human soul that has been cut off from its true grounding, no longer part of a much larger nature. Under those circumstances, it should come as no surprise to read that we were commanded by a jealous, very hard-to-please warrior-God to subdue and dominate nature (Gen.1:28).

No wonder, then, that from this Hebrew context there would eventually arise another religion, Christianity, that focused even more on the sense of separation and estrangement, to the point of declaring that only a supernatural act of God could save us from ourselves. The feeling of alienation that lies at the heart of male-dominated cultures forms the base of patriarchy and the perverse view of nature as something foreign or inferior to us. It was then left to the promoters of this view to explain in their own terms how it came about.

Note: An excellent modern translation of the Hebrew version of the creation story is to be found in *Hebrew Myths: The Book of Genesis*, by Robert Graves and Raphael Patai. New York: McGraw-Hill, 1963).

Chapter Two

Perversion

The invention of original sin ruled out a positive attitude toward nature, including our own.

In their efforts to explain the sense of separation that they themselves created, worshipers of the victorious goddess-slaying god invented the notion of original sin. Developing ideas to be found in Essene Judaism, the Christian apostle Paul and his followers promoted the fantastic belief that every human born since the "fall into sin" resulting from the first man's disobedience (the man being led to it by the woman at the suggestion of the snake, long a symbol of goddess-centered religion) is to be held equally responsible! "Sin came into the world through one man (Adam) and death through sin, and so death spread to all men because all men sinned" (Romans 5:12).

It requires a large leap of logic to believe that, since sin and death came into the world at the beginning of the human adventure, all people born since must have sinned—or, as Paul concluded, are sinful by nature. We search in vain for an explanation of the mechanism by which all humans have inherited Adam's sin. Yet that assertion is simply stated as if it were a fact. Somehow, having to die means that you deserve it, and worse.

Paul's position was elaborated upon by theologians such as Augustine, Aquinas, Luther, Calvin, and Jonathan Edwards. Their view would have us look upon our newborn children as so full of wickedness that they deserve everlasting punishment—unless "saved." It should be clear that the offer of salvation is meaningless without the assumption concerning what one is being saved from: one's own sinful nature.

God is said to be our "Father." What would we think of a human father who would punish his child, even momentarily, simply for having been born? How can so many millions of people have accepted this degrading doctrine? Many Christians don't believe it. Some are quoted in this book. However, people who do believe it are on the increase worldwide. The present trend of world Christianity as a whole is moving in the direction of an anti-intellectual, ego-centered fundamentalism. It would be foolish to ignore the implications of this unfortunate development and evasive to fail to address it.

Near the end of his life, when he was dying of cancer, the most influential student of the human mind in modern times, Sigmund Freud, arrived at much the same sort of conclusion as did those religious folk whose beliefs he disdained. He invented a "death wish," with which we are all presumably born. He did this out of a deep disappointment (his *Civilization and Its Discontents* makes this clear) and a clinical failure to understand masochism: the need that some sick people have to hurt themselves. He decided that sadism—the need to hurt others, especially in a sexual way—is somehow an outgrowth of masochism, the presumed inborn wish for one's own destruction. There is no evidence that newborns come into the world with any such desire. They will struggle for life and do whatever they can to avoid pain.

Freud's youngest and liveliest co-worker, Wilhelm Reich, got it right. After successfully treating a case of masochism, he saw that efforts to harm oneself stem from the turning inward of rage and a need for revenge against whoever caused the distress. Reich saw that the underlying feeling of masochism is a fear of "bursting," which arises from an inability to tolerate uncontrollable movements of energy in one's own body. No wonder, then, that masochistic behavior is controlled behavior, with the practitioner often giving explicit directions. Keeping life-energy from getting out of control is the issue. But the masochist is doomed to failure, life-energy being spontaneous by nature.

There is no good reason to think that we were born bad in either the religious or psychological sense. Having a positive view of human nature, even in the face of the ills of the world, is an important part of healing what ails us.

Chapter Three

Doctrine

The doctrine of atonement further turned us against ourselves.

From the Trinitarian Christian point of view, the Bible's "old story of salvation" centers around the idea of atonement: "For God so loved the world that He gave His only Son, that whoever believes in him should not perish but have eternal life" (John 3:16 - the most quoted sentence in the Christian Bible, written at least 60 years after Jesus' death). As welcome as this offer of salvation may seem, the assumptions underlying it are too rarely mentioned or understood. The issue becomes clearer when the idea of salvation is coupled with the usual heaven-or-hell consequence of belief or lack of it.

The Russian philosopher, Nikolai Berdyaev, called the belief in hell "the most disgusting morality ever conceived." Why such strong language regarding a widespread conviction of sincere believers? Consider the assumption on which that belief is based. For two centuries, Trinitarian Christians have insisted that there is a huge gap between us and God: because we are so sinful, and God is so good. They say it was His graceful decision to send His son to live as one of us and suffer and die in our place. Only by so doing could He forgive us for having inherited Adam's sinfulness; otherwise, we deserve a hellish future. That is their idea of God's love.

Their idea of divine sympathy is for God to enter human life one time for about thirty years, at the end of which the God-man suffers for a few hours, dies, appears to a few chosen people, and then returns to his heavenly home, leaving in his place an immaterial spirit as "comforter." Considering the immense amount of human suffering that occurs every hour on this earth, that brief moment in history can have little other than symbolic significance.

How can one man's suffering be conceived as an actual atonement for the suffering—or misdeeds, or "fallen nature"—of every single other human being? Rather than make sense of it, holders of that believe tell us that it must be accepted as a matter of faith.

Rather than engage in the futility of trying to understand something that makes no sense, we may ask, as the Universalist Hosea Ballou did: who, other than a psychopathic human father, would ever think of having his only son killed as a means of righting some wrong? Even the first patriarch of Judaism, Abraham, was supposed to hear a voice telling him there must be a better way, and a substitute was provided. But only after he was willing to kill his son. Sacrifice of first-born sons was common in Old Testament times, even among the Hebrews. "The first-born of thy sons shalt thou give to Me" (Exodus 22:28). Common preaching upholds Abraham's willingness to sacrifice his son, Isaac, as a sign of his great faith. The Danish philosopher, Sören Kierkegaard, summed up that point of view in his commentary on the Abraham-Isaac story: "True sacrifice is to act contrary to one's deepest feeling." And "Faith begins precisely where thinking leaves off." I hope the reader will consider as preferable, the Unitarian, Albert Schweitzer's view: "*Renunciation of thinking is a declaration of spiritual bankruptcy.*"

An important assumption underlying the atonement-by-means-of-sacrifice doctrine is that God, being omnipotent, knows our feelings, but He doesn't actually feel them. That would seem to be beneath his dignity. God may want what's best for us and even care about us in some parental sense, but being an absentee father and not directly approachable, he doesn't directly share in our pleasures or sufferings. Therefore, he must provide an intermediary. That important assumption should be questioned, as there is an intelligible and more ethically sound alternative viewpoint that upholds the belief that God actually does love the world. This topic is offered in Part IV.

Chapter Four

Omnipotence and Predestination

An all-powerful God would be a tyrant who has ruled out a world of decision-making people. Theological predestination is no better than materialistic determinism. They both impede an adequate understanding of nature.

"We do not honor God by breaking down the human soul, connecting it with him only by a tie of slavish dependence. It is his glory that he creates beings like himself, free beings . . . that he confers on them the reality, not the show, of power."
~William Ellery Channing (1788-1842) Leader of American Unitarianism in the early 19th century

"Omnipotence . . . is a false or indeed absurd ideal, which in truth LIMITS God, denies to him any world worth talking about: a world of . . . decision-making agents." *~Charles Hartshorne (1897-2001) "Creative Process" Philosophical Theologian*

A social worker, who worked with abused and neglected children, wrote a strongly worded article in which he noted that the pedophile crisis in the church is centered on an inexcusable abuse of power. Speaking of the abuser-priests, he noted that "Many of us were told from a young age that these men were the 'representatives on earth' of an 'all-knowing, all-powerful' God. We imagined they could do no wrong."[1] No wonder, then, that the abusers were able to use their privileged positions to gain the trust of their victims. That is what can come of belief in a god who is all-powerful and all-knowing, and who, if he is to be obeyed, must have earthly enforcers of his will.

One of the ironies of religious history is that the prevailing Christian concept of God as perfect and unchanging, all-powerful and all-knowing, was founded more on Greek philosophy than on the Bible. Classical Christian theology is based on the philosophical determinism that the Christian writers found in Greek philosophy. That determinism logically rules out any real free will or human choice, not to mention spontaneity in the rest of creation. That theology upholds a tyrant-god, free of direct involvement, except for a brief thirty years, who cannot tolerate novelty and who has turned human life into a puppet show that he plays for his own amusement.

The most influential Roman Catholic theologian, Thomas Aquinas, reasoned that if God is perfect in power, then whatever happens is divinely made to happen, and whatever will happen must be eternally known to God. This implies that, for God, there is no open future and that, since God knows all our thoughts and actions in advance, they have already been decided. The Protestant, John Calvin, reasoned in much the same manner.

Ironically, this "predestination" idea that forms the core of the theology of Calvin and Jonathan Edwards, is logically compatible with the deterministic philosophy of materialism, which holds that terms like "chance," or "possibility," "time," "change," and "purpose" have no real meaning since reality is all "cause and effect." If the future has already been determined by an omnipotent and omniscient God- or by the strict *cause-and-effect* logic of material processes, in the case of scientific materialism—then there is no possibility. Nothing is left to chance or choice; past, present and future are all the same in the mind of God; creative change is an illusion; and "purpose" (which depends upon the possibility of its not being fulfilled) is an absurdity. In such a world, there is no point to people having purposes in the first place.

People who are concerned about their own individual salvation are then caught in an impossible double-bind: they should feel responsible for their "choice"—*for or against* the grace of God, which alone can enable one to make the saving decision—when, according to their doctrine, the decision to give or withhold that grace had been made long before they were born.

There are hints of predestination in the Essene Jewish Dead Sea Scrolls and in Paul's letters, but Jesus spoke of a *God of Mercy*—some scholars prefer "compassion,"—another concept that determinism deprives of all meaning. An all-knowing, all-powerful God doesn't change his mind. The God of the Bible does, many times.

Fausto Sozzini (1539-1604), an Italian who developed the first Unitarian theology as the intellectual leader of the Minor Reformed Church of Poland (and thus is better known by the Polish name: Faustus Socinus), saw that predestination is the tyrant ideal of power: "I decide. You only THINK you decide." Such determinism contradicts a merciful God of love, who gives real freedom in a world of choice and chance, as well as cause and effect.

Much has been said and written about the existence of evil in the world often without noting that the essence of evil is the need to control, to have power over others. Any god worthy of our worship would have no such desire. "We cannot bow before a being, however great and powerful, who governs tyrannically . . . We venerate, not the loftiness of God's throne, but the equity and goodness in which it is established," said William Ellery Channing in his famous sermon on Unitarian Christianity.

How may we understand the power of God if not according to the supernatural conception? This question will be addressed in Part IV. In order to clear the way for more positive concepts, we need, first, to understand why other popular points of view are either incorrect or inadequate. Let us now turn to Humanism.

[1]Peter Pollard, "Clerical abuse: a case against forgiving or forgetting." *Boston Globe*, 4/7/02.

Chapter Five

Humanism

To the extent that it slights feeling and thinking in the non-human world and fails to address our long-term future, humanism represents a dead end in human thinking. Natural religion makes up for this inadequacy.

Charles Hartshorne began his book, *Beyond Humanism*, written in 1937 with these words: "In the best sense, 'humanism' is simply the expression of an interest in man; in the worst sense, this interest becomes a monomania, excluding interest in anything else. Insofar as it develops such exclusiveness, humanism contradicts its own intent, for interest in man implies interest in those things in which man is interested; and in what is man not interested? Darwin devoted himself to the study of earthworms; the astronomer gives heed to objects inconceivably remote in space-time. To indicate the scope of human interest we must speak with Plato of 'all time and existence.'"[1]

Humanism points to the highest human attributes—love, justice, mercy and the like—as the nearest thing to the divine that we know of, but, to the extent that it conceives human beings as the pinnacle of creation, it puts us in an indefensible and presumptuous position. Given what we now know about the existence of other planetary systems in the Universe, it is unlikely that we humans represent the most developed form of intelligence—and our ethical behavior as a species certainly leaves much to be desired.

Humanism, as it is usually conceived, shares with supernaturalism the same error: they both treat nature, in its nonhuman aspects, as unfeeling and unthinking and of little, if any, ethical significance. The importance of recognizing emotion and intelligence in the non-human world will be highlighted in Parts III and IV of this book.

The problem of treating nature as unfeeling and unintelligent is symbolized in the heretofore-mentioned creation myth of separation, which, by severing the earthly from the heavenly, isolates matter from feeling, mind and purpose. We have seen some of the theological ramifications undergirding this point of view. To make matters worse, modern science has been seen to support it: with the materialistic doctrine of simple cause and effect, with no room for either feeling or thought anywhere except in animals with brains. How such material objects as brains can either feel or think is a problem that some neuroscientists believe is being solved in concert with a materialist philosophy. This philosophical assumption calls for critical examination as we shall see in the third part of this book.

Humanism is preferable to a supernaturalism that worships a tyrant god. But humanism also represents a "dead end" in human thinking. Why? Consider our natural interest in the future. In the long term, we can expect the eventual extinction of humankind unless we are able to colonize other star systems, a remote possibility at best. We may extinguish ourselves long before the earth is destroyed. So we must look forward to a time when all human achievements will be as if they had never been. That's a depressing thought. Of course, we may choose not to think it. If we were another sort of animal, we wouldn't be burdened with such a thought. But it is reasonable that, once in a while, we should become concerned about our long-term future, both as a species and as individuals.

If we ask about what lasts from our past, we are led to ponder the effects on others of our deeds, plus the preservation of our past through our memory of it. When all our life is in the past, what then? What will be its significance? We will not know it, unless our consciousness survives. Others may know it for a while, but not for very long. In what sense, then, will our lives, feelings, thoughts, and accomplishments still be fact?

Even if you don't believe in somehow surviving death, you are still not left without a positive alternative. It is that everything we contribute to life, especially of a loving sort, will not be lost when we die. I will take up that assertion in the fourth part of this book.

[1]Charles Hartshorne, *Beyond Humanism*. Chicago: Willet, Clark & Co., 1941.

Chapter Six

Can Religion Be Natural?

The traditional assumption that faith comes before understanding is ill-founded and should be rejected. Knowledge of the natural world can lead us to the truth about God.

As clear-headed as he was concerning the logical and ethical trap of belief in an omnipotent and omniscient God, the Unitarian, Socinus, was shackled by a strictly Biblical backing for his beliefs. This led him to deny that there can be a nature-derived knowledge of God or valid natural theology.

That point of view is upheld by theologians to this day, including many of the liberals. They maintain that faith both precedes and enables understanding and that, therefore, one can never gain knowledge of God by means of any encounter with the natural world. A natural theology must reject that principle. An approach to religion that is compatible with scientific thinking must see understanding as primary and faith as secondary.

Any faith worth having **must** be based on understanding because it is not possible, in actuality, to believe in something that one does not understand. Understanding is based on something more solid than faith can ever be: observation and evidence. Isn't that why orthodox Christians insist on the veracity of the presumed witnesses to Jesus' resurrection? If there is NO evidence for that belief, of what use is faith? We might as well believe in whatever we want.

How is it possible for someone to believe something that he or she cannot understand? People may say they "have faith," and that includes "believing in" something (like the Trinity or salvation through atonement) that they can't explain because they don't understand it—but they still "believe" it! The assertion rings hollow. Isn't it better to build our religion on experience and understanding?

The relationship between belief and understanding is similar to that of love and knowledge. How is it possible to love someone whom you do not know? It isn't. It is not possible genuinely to love another person without caring for his or her well-being, which necessarily includes an understanding of that person's needs and desires. That is why those cult leaders who attract gullible followers in the name of "Love" are so destructive. Their real goal is to control others–as their methods show. Focusing on the division between the saved and the damned, they try to convince prospective members that they are only trying to save them. But it turns out to be a matter of "follow the leader." I think of Rev. Moon's "Unification Church" and his obedient followers. I once took the trouble to read his theological book, *The Divine Principle*, and was appalled that any intelligent person could possibly accept such nonsensical self-promotion, all at the expense of others. Anyone who offers salvation or a life of love and peace and service to others at the price of relinquishing responsibility for your own life is a fake. Control is the goal. Can you think of a religion based on supernaturalism where human control of other humans is not rationalized as a necessary part of the arrangement? (The typical recruitment explains why some "fall" to fake religions: leaders strategize and seek out people who may be at their most vulnerable times of life—first year of college, a hospitalization, a holiday alone, and so on. We must, therefore, sympathize with those who are taken in.)

That nature and people are often destructive does not invalidate natural religion or a theology based upon the revelation of God in nature, rather than by means of a book or the teachings of a church. Ample evidence of natural destruction requires intelligent explanation if we are to claim ethical soundness for the natural view. That believer must be able to make sense of disastrous "acts of God" and cruel human behavior and waste of life. I will explain how natural religion encourages healthful human community and sound ethical thinking and moral behavior and address these characteristics of natural religion in Parts IV and V.

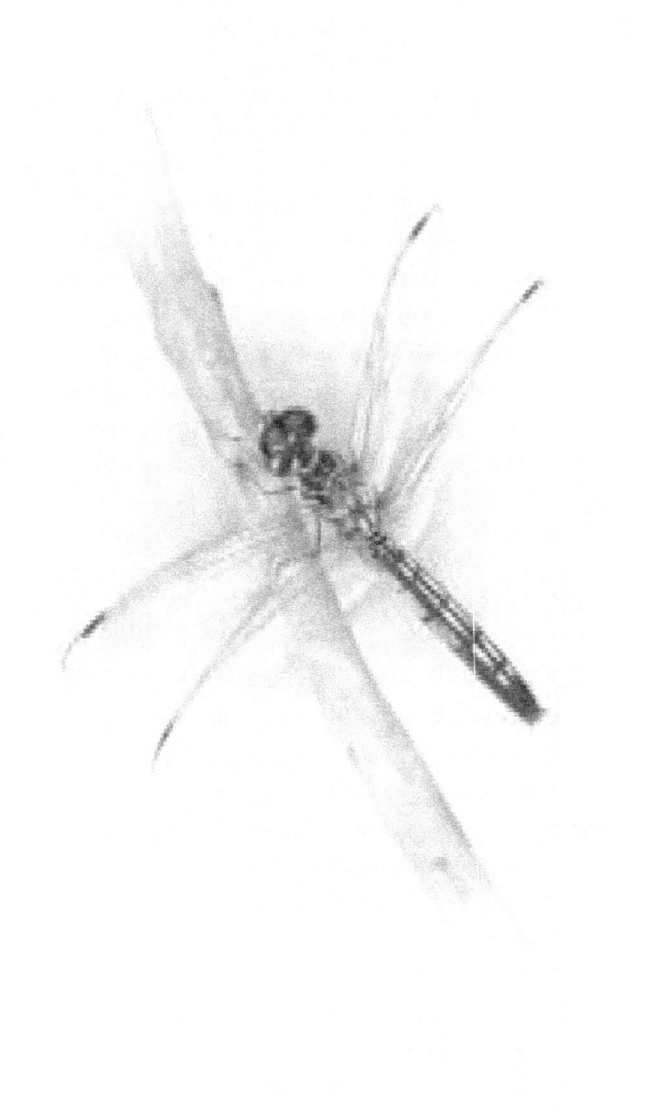

PART II
SEPARATION AND CONNECTION IN RELIGIONS

The usual approach to the religions of the world is to treat them according to the notion of progress from "primitive" (such as Native American) to "advanced" (such as Christianity). Whether genuine progress has actually been made is open to serious question especially when it comes to the crucial issue of *separation and connection*. Let's take a fresh look at the various religions and focus on this issue with the caveat that I neither intend to nor pretend to offer a comprehensive view of any of the religions under consideration.

Chapter One

Animistic Religions

Animism should not be disparaged–but better understood, because it links humans with nature.

"The soul of the universe is never seen. Its voice alone is heard . . . a gentle voice like a woman, a voice so fine and gentle that even children cannot become afraid. What it says is 'be not afraid of the universe.'" ~*Alaskan Eskimo, quoted by Knud Rasmussen*

In modern times, almost all scientists have operated on the materialistic assumption that nature is a giant mechanism that is largely lifeless and that there is no such thing as spirit or any sort of energy specific to life. Even so, our English word "animal" comes from "anima," Latin for "soul." Up through the medieval period, it was believed that all animate creatures had souls. However, the soul was not something inside the body; rather, the body was in the soul, which permeated all parts of the body. This implies a connection between human life and the life of animate nature.

When God Was a Woman

The patriarchal suppression of the old goddess religion has caused much mischief —especially with respect to the treatment of women. Patriarchy has separated us from nature.

"The Eternal Feminine draws us on." ~*Goethe*

Long before the sacred scriptures of the world were written, prehistoric ("primitive") human beings found the entire world suffused with sacred powers, the supreme symbol of which was the Goddess. Archaeologists such as Marija Gimbutas have shown that the ultimate religious symbol—"God" in patriarchal cultures—was originally (and for about thirty thousand years) feminine.

I refer the reader to the writings of Joseph Campbell for elucidation of many important implications of this realization. My purpose is to emphasize the loss of connection that inevitably came about with the deliberate suppression of goddess-oriented religion. The Bible is one of several religious documents that have perpetuated the calculated distortion by males of the female principle, a manipulative process that is symbolized by the triumph of the patriarchal deities of the sky cults over the matriarchal deities of the earth.

The natural concept is that of the Earth-Mother, the womb from which all living things are born and to which all return. There developed on earth a feeling and conception of the woman, especially during her time of pregnancy and menstruation, as the center and source of an effective magical force. In the earliest ages of human community, the power and wonder of the female was no less a marvel than was the universe itself. It was the Great Mother to whom sacrifices were made and prayers addressed. It was the priesthood of women who practiced the magical arts of healing and prophecy. The Great Mother Goddess, incarnation of the life-force, reigned over sky, earth and underworld and revealed Herself to humankind in the ever-renewing productivity of the earth and ever recurring rhythms of the new, full, and waning moon. Her subordinate male consort was the young god, alternatively her son and her lover, who died with the harvest and was reborn with the spring seed. And woman, who shared the magic of procreation and nurture, whose menstrual cycle coincided with the lunar cycle, was the link in this cosmic drama of fertility.

Why did the male leaders of the patriarchal cults expend so much energy suppressing the truly old-time religion? Why have we been taught that Eve, the mother of humanity, was fashioned from Adam's rib and was called "woman" because she was taken from a man? Why are we taught by our Judeo-Christian heritage that humankind's tragic expulsion from the Garden of Eden and all our ensuing earthly travail we owe to the first woman, who was tempted by a snake, ate the forbidden fruit, and then tempted Adam and caused the Fall? Why did God tell her that her "desire shall be to thy husband, and he shall rule over thee."

Why did St. Paul declare the husband to be the "head" of the wife even as Christ is head of the church? Why have theologians taught that woman was made in the image of man, and not God, as man was? Why does the Muslim Koran proclaim the superiority of men to women (Surah IV: 34: "Men are in charge of women, because Allah hath made the one of them to excel the other, and because they spend of their property for the support of women. So good women are the obedient, guarding in secret that which Allah hath guarded)—as do the Hindu Laws of Manu, which insist that the wife must worship the husband "as a god?"

Why did the Greek mythologists turn Pandora, who originally was the source of all good gifts as one of the earliest earth-goddesses, into a wily seductress, who ensnared men and brought gifts of sorrow to humankind? Why did Nammu, the Sumerian goddess of the sea, the primal generative force of the world, become "chaos," eventually the chaos of Genesis, which the male Yaweh split and shaped to His ends, and which, in Greek philosophy, succumbed to the male order? And why, in Catholic Christianity, is a woman elevated to the position of Mother of God only as a virgin?

Why is there a Jewish prayer that men of old recited, "Thank you, God, for not making me a woman."

Why have women and femininity been so despised and degraded in religion and culture?

The Hebrew scripture (Christian "Old Testament") refers often to "idols." Those "idols" were held sacred in the goddess religions. They included the serpent which, because it was seen to slough off its skin and seemed to live forever, was associated with the life-giving force of the earth-mother-goddess. The transformation of the serpent into a symbol of temptation and evil represents a deliberate denigration of women and elevation of male supremacy and patriarchal social structure. The horns of the bull were seen to represent the phases of the moon, linked with the maiden-nurturer-crone phases of a woman's life, and the bull also came to represent the goddess' male consort. The bull's blood was shed in some cults so that man might have life and have it more abundantly. Moses had it smashed. In the Hebrew Bible, the Ashtareth are symbols of the goddess, Ashtar, Queen of Heaven, to whom sacrifices were made by "heathens." She was "the abomination." Worship of her was eliminated.

Despite representing, in some ways, a creative advance in religion, the religion of the Hebrew Bible was, in large part, a rationalization of a reactionary force, which elevated patriarchy. The important exception is the work of the prophets, who spoke eloquently of a god of justice.

Tremendous energy has been expended to overcome the older, more natural religion. And much of human culture is terribly wounded as a result. This wounded-ness is made evident by the prevalence of rape and other forms of abuse of women in our culture. According to the National Victim Center, a woman is raped every minute in the United States. A university study found that over half of the male students surveyed acknowledged that they would commit rape if they thought they could get away with it. Domestic violence is the leading cause of injury to women ages 15 to 44 in the United States. These are examples of the price of patriarchy.

The development of men's secret societies may be understood as a reaction against the old-time religion when the secrets of the kingdom of the goddess were known only to women who kept their own centers of worship that no man dare approach. Traditionally in Native American societies, women are forbidden to enter the men's lodge or tent during religious ceremonies because it is said that they will "contaminate" the worship. From a Jewish or Christian perspective it is assumed that this is because the women are "dirty" as in the Old Testament law that menstruating women must be isolated. Consider also the Russian Orthodox teaching that a woman is "unclean" for forty days after childbirth and cannot even be present when the infant is baptized. Baptism, in the orthodox view, amounts to an initiation into the Kingdom of the Father by "cleansing" the inborn "sinfulness" of the infant (or adolescent, in some Christian communities). It is intended to sanitize a natural female function (childbirth) and, of course, the sexual function that brought pregnancy. Baptism thus stems from an age-old fear: the fear of women's natural power.

Living closer to nature and more in harmony with it, Native Americans have taught that the "contamination" of the male ritual by the women's presence has nothing to do with dirtiness, but, rather, is an acknowledgment of their natural power—mystery to the men—which the men can only try to "drum up" by their contrived ceremonies. The men dress up in all sorts of impressive costumes, and their representations of the gods are likewise ceremonially clothed. The Goddess needs no dress. She is naked - because her power is natural.

Both civilization and warfare were "advanced" (there must be a better term) and patriarchy developed in earnest when the agricultural villages were attacked and raided by nomadic bands of crude characters who took over with their weapons and male gods. Joseph Campbell tells the story of how the men broke the magical power of the women by contriving a mythology that honors God by keeping women in the kitchen. The men formed their own secret societies, which included rituals such as the "sub-incision" practice, whereby, in addition to circumcision, a slit was cut under the initiate's scrotum to resemble a vagina: "We too can bleed and not die." What better example of the wounding of which the Grail myth speaks?

The belief that the spiritual is opposed to the earthly is a man-made invention, stemming from fear of the female power and the desire forcefully to suppress it. Rupture from the mother is the primary motif in male puberty rites. Among some tribes, the initiate was made to tread over his mother's belly to symbolize the severance. Through initiation, the novice underwent a ritual death unto the maternal "profane" universe and was "reborn" into the paternal "spiritual" realm of the Father. "*I and the Father are One*" did not originate with Jesus. Shedding and drinking the father's blood as a means of cementing the Father-Son relationship is an ancient practice.

The first gods were born from the bodies of goddesses. When the men took over, both gods and goddesses were then conceived unnaturally, like Athena from the head of Zeus, and the whole world from the brain—and by means of the mouth of Yaweh. Creation by a mental act symbolizes the dominance of the brain over the body and the mental over the physical, which might not be so bad if it didn't also involve a degradation of the sexual function.

A telling image of this perversion is that of the Virgin Mary (common on Catholic prayer cards) stepping on a serpent (following Genesis 2:15: "And you shall bruise his heel"). Here we have a complete reversal: the old symbol of immortality and the energy of life closely associated with the Goddess is transformed into a dreadful symbol of evil—and is trampled by the one remaining feminine divinity, the Mother of God—now a virgin, however, because it is believed that God's Son can only emerge from a love that does not involve sex. Why is this obvious denigration of woman and of the sexual function so rarely recognized as such?

Yet, even within these degrading traditions, there remain reminders of life-affirming religion. In the 15th century, an anonymous woodcarver created a little statue of Mother and Child—"Vierge Ovurante"—that Joseph Campbell used to love to show. It has a door in the front that, when opened, reveals images of the Father, Son and Holy Spirit—the entire Trinity—all enclosed within the body of the Mother!

African Rhythm

The religious sensibility common to the nations of Africa assumes a direct connection with nature.

"Primitive" or "animistic" religions, like those native to the countries of the African continent, are usually excluded from study of world religions because of the presumed superiority of "higher-level" religions, like Hinduism and Christianity. That this presumption is evidence of an anti-nature attitude should be obvious, but it seems to have escaped almost all of the writers of books regarding religions.

Indigenous peoples had the experience of having one of the higher religions —in the personage of Christian missionaries—come and say, "We want to teach you how to pray. Now close your eyes." And when they opened their eyes, their land had been taken.[1] Christianity is now viewed by many there as an attempt to quench their spirit for the purpose of political and economic gain for the white man.

Islam, not a white man's religion and without colonialist associations, has gained ground in parts of Africa, as elsewhere in the world. But, to many people of African countries, Islam is still a foreign religion as it is based on a book, rather than on nature.

Jack Mendelssohn wrote about a Native who spoke of his rejection of both Christianity and Communism: "Communism would want to suppress the rhythm, that vital force, in me. Colonialism tried to do the same thing. Christianity tried to do the same thing. Both failed. Communism is going to fail too. There is something deep in me which hates drabness, . . . Without the vital force, the rhythm, . . . how would I survive?"[1]

The beautiful multitude of African religions makes little sense to the critical mind because they are based on feeling more than thought. A felt connection with other living things—the feeling of life-energy itself—is considered more important than an understanding of life. It is direct contact with the vital force, the "rhythm" that counts.

The whole world is alive! And there is rhythm to all things! That is the essence of religion for them. Without this sense of aliveness and rhythm, everything is drab, dull, lifeless. Westerners may dismiss this attitude with the pejorative term, "animism." But what, after all, is animism but the awareness of our being part of a much larger unity of living things, a "rhythmic system" of felt relationships? Does not our modern physics say that energy lies at the heart of all things and that all things are in some sense related? The scientist tries to understand things; the "animist" feels them.

Then, when trying to understand the world, the Native African came to believe in a great Creator God: "The One you meet everywhere," "giver of breath and souls." God is rhythmic energy in everything, often conceived in both male and female terms. No temples exist to God, yet few doubt God's existence. Why build temples when God is everywhere and you may worship God under the open sky? But then, why try to worship God (whom no one has ever seen, as Jesus said) directly when you may worship any number of the God-created spirits who concern themselves directly with human affairs? How different is that view from that of Hindus who pray to numerous gods and goddesses or that of Christian believers who pray to the Virgin or to the saints?

[1] Jack Mendelssohn, *God, Allah, and Juju*. Boston: Beacon Press, 1962, p. 21.
[2] Mendelssohn, p. 228.

Native American Religion

We have much to learn about diversity and relatedness from this great spiritual tradition.

"We know that the white man does not understand our ways. One portion of land is the same to him as the next, for he is a stranger who comes in the night and takes from the land whatever he needs. The earth is not his kin, but his enemy, and when he has conquered it, he moves on . . . He treats his mother, the earth, and his brother, the sky, as things to be bought, plundered, sold like sheep or bright beads. His appetite will devour the earth and leave behind only a desert . . . There is no quiet place in the white city . . . What is there to life if a person cannot hear the lonely cry of the whippoorwill or the arguments of the frogs around a pond at night? . . . The air is precious to the Red, for all things share the same breath . . . The White does not seem to notice the air he breathes. Like a man dying for many days, he is numb to the stench . . . What is humanity without the beasts? If all the beasts were gone, we would die from a great loneliness of spirit. For whatever happens to the beasts soon happens to us. All things are connected . . . You may think now that you own God as you wish to own our land; but you cannot . . . The earth is precious to God, and to harm the earth is to heap contempt on its creator." ~*Chief Seattle, leader of the Suquamish tribe in the Washington territory, marking the transferal of ancestral Indian lands to the federal government in 1854*

NATURAL RELIGION

What is life? It is the flash of a firefly in the night. It is the breath of a buffalo in the wintertime. It is the little shadow which runs across the grass and loses itself in the sunset.
~*Last words of Crowfoot, Orator for the Blackfoot Confederacy*

One summer in the early 1980s, I visited an archeological dig that was taking place a mile from my summer cabin in Maine. The artifacts had been dated at about eleven thousand years. I was fortunate to discover, between my bare toes, a Clovis spear-point. As I felt it, and looked at it, I thought about what it might have meant for people to be living there so long ago and what life was like for the people. It is clear that they knew how to survive under conditions that we would find intolerable. They probably had some religion although we'll never know the scope of it. They were the forebears of those Native Americans we call Indians, owing to Columbus' mistaken impression.

Columbus Day is the only U.S. national holiday that honors a foreigner who never set foot on our land and who murdered and enslaved many Native Central Americans. A few years ago (I write this in 2019), I convinced the Durham, New Hampshire Town Council to declare Columbus Day Indigenous Peoples Day, the first community in our state to do so, thereby joining many cities and a few states in that growing recognition.

No one knows how many Native Americans lived on the two continents in 1492. The figure ranges from 15 to 80 million. We do know that their cultures were devastated and most of their people were killed, died of imported diseases, or shipped to Europe as slaves. As Joseph Campbell lamented, "Four hundred years after

[Columbus'] landing, the native order of culture and life in the Western Hemisphere was extinct. There has never been anything like it in the history of the planet. Like a plague, the virus of Christian love went across the continents, leaving in its wake museums -where there had formerly been populations."[1]

In 1779, George Washington ordered General Sullivan to wipe the Iroquois from the face of the earth: "Not to be merely overrun, but destroyed." In 1794, the first U.S. treaty with a foreign nation was signed with the Six Nations of the Iroquois Confederacy to establish peaceful relations and reservations for Indians. It was to last forever. It was broken with the building of the Kinzua dam in the 1960s that devastated the culture of the Senecas who inhabited that region.

In 1862, on the same day that he signed the Emancipation Proclamation, Abraham Lincoln signed a death warrant for Dakota Sioux who were already starving. In 1880, a U.S. Congressman summed up the prevailing conqueror's attitude: "Congress must apprise the Indian that he can no longer stand as a backwater against the constantly swelling tide of civilization. An idle and thriftless race of savages cannot be permitted to stand guard at the treasure vaults which hold our gold and silver." And, in 1884, the U.S. Supreme Court declared that an "Indian" is by birth an "alien" (!) and a dependent of the government. Native American religions were outlawed under the federal Civilization Regulations from the 1880s to the 1930s. All the traditional religions were driven underground, some to the point of extinction. They were even forbidden to sing their sacred songs, and many were executed for so doing. Some 90 million acres of native land was taken by the federal government—all without compensation. Native Americans lost 98% of their land base.

All such events happened as a result of a set of beliefs held by the conquerors that is deeply imbedded in our religious heritage: an outlook that is the polar opposite of that of native peoples all over the world. Richard Slotkin's book, *Regeneration Through Violence: The Mythology of the American Frontier*, offers a good understanding of the confrontation between two diametrically different cultures, modes of perception, and visions of the nature and destiny of humankind. For example, he tells of an incident when a Native American asked to shake the hand of a missionary as a signal of mutual respect. The missionary ". . . rose hastily from his seat and replied that he could not do so since there could be no fellowship between the religion of God and the works of the devil" (Richard Slotkin, *Regeneration Through Violence*. Middletown, CT: Wesleyan Press, 1973). Of all the anticipated perils to the white conquerors, that of "Indian cannibals" evoked the strongest emotions in good Christian folk—who drank the blood and ate the body of their God every Sunday. What's more, the savages didn't believe in sin.

In recent times, some descendants of the white conquerors have gained an appreciation of the spirituality of native peoples. The liberal Catholic cultural historian Thomas Berry calls the Indian form of nature mysticism ". . . one of the most integral forms of spirituality known to us . . . This is precisely the mystique that is of utmost necessity at the present time to reorient the consciousness of the present occupants of the North American continent toward a reverence for the earth, so urgent if the bio-systems of the continent are to survive."[2]

Native American versions of creation typically have the first people emerging from the earth and hungering for something better. Whereas the Christian myth deplores our Fall and urges us to improve on nature, the native myths rejoice in the discovery of and movement into a nurturing world. To the native, the world is divine, whether its face is at the moment good or ill. It deserves our respect for both its beauty and its cruelty. All living things are relatives. There is no split between humanity and the rest of creation, no division between "us" and "them," the saved and the damned, as there is in the Judeo-Christian-Muslim tradition.

The primary task of native religions is to determine the proper relationship that people must have with all living things. Rather than subduing and dominating the world as the Bible commands believers to do, the native recognizes his dependence on and relationship with everything in creation. All are brothers and sisters. Each form of life has its own purpose and a unique quality to its existence. As a Sioux Indian has said, "The reason Wakan Tanka does not make two birds or animals or human beings exactly alike is that each is placed here by Wakan Tanka to be an independent individuality and to rely upon itself."

"Primitive" religions, like those of Native American sovereign nations, have too often been dismissed as lacking in sophistication. Nothing could be further from the truth, as any serious student of the rituals of the Hopis, for example, knows. The great Dakota man of knowledge, Black Elk, expressed a profound realization when he said that God is the Center of the Universe, and that this

Center is actually everywhere, within each and every living being. His assertion echoed a similar statement, by a 12th century Christian mystic who said that "God is an intelligible sphere whose center is everywhere and circumference nowhere."[3] Such a sense of the sacred can only come from a deep feeling of contact with the natural world.

[1] Joseph Campbell, *Historical Atlas of World Mythology*, Vol. II, Part 3. NY: Harper and Row, 1989, p. 307.
[2] Thomas Berry, *The Dream of the Earth*. San Francisco: Sierra Club Books, 1998, p. 184.
[3] Quoted by Joseph Campbell in his *Myths to Live By*, and elsewhere.

Shinto:
The Binding Relationship

This Japanese religion - minus the emperor worship - emphasizes the human connection to the natural world.

"There is no place on this whole earth that is not a shrine, be it the ocean's vast expanse or wildest mountain peak, sun-caressed. In all things resides the ever-present power-divine . . . Even in the single leaf of a tree, or a tender blade of grass, the awe-inspiring Deity manifests itself."
~*Senge-Takazumi (1797-1875)*

Joseph Campbell liked to tell the story of a group of American clergymen who visited some Shinto shrines and temples in Japan. After a while, one of them grew impatient and said to the Shinto priest: "I don't get it. I've seen all these things and heard your words, but I don't get your theology. What's your theology?" The priest smiled and replied: "We don't have theology. We dance."[1]

My study and practice of Aikido, a Japanese martial art that may seem a sort of dance[2] awakened my interest in Shinto, which Westerners usually associate with Emperor-worship - an aspect of the religion that has lost most of its relevance. It may seem condescending for me to include Shinto as an "animistic" religion, yet I mean it as compliment.

Shinto is called "the Way of the Gods," or, better, "a

way of walking." The Japanese term for Shinto means "up the mountain." Because of living close to nature—never more than 70 miles from the ocean, with many mountains covering 80% of the land and, therefore, visible from nearly every vantage point, and a fairly friendly climate—the Japanese early came to believe in an intimate linkage between what is inside and what is outside the human person. Shi-kata is "the way of doing things," with emphasis on the form and order of the process, rather than focusing on results. The point of all of the various "katas"—for eating properly, for using the telephone, for exchanging business cards, for dealing with non-Japanese, and so on—is to be in harmony with the natural way of doing things.

There are in Shinto millions of kami - usually translated as "gods" or "spirits"—invisible, mysterious, and to be respected, since they provide the power for growth and creativity, helping us to "walk onward." Shinto is unusual in conceiving of the sun, not as a god, but as a goddess, Amateratzu - whose naughty brother caused mischief that led her to hide for a while in a cave, until lured out by dancing. "We don't have theology: we dance."

Perceptive Japanese understand that even this highest goddess is but a manifestation of the divine spirit that is in all things - and, therefore, all things are to be regarded as divine. This is God *in* nature rather than a being separate from nature.

The primary metaphor through which Shinto sees the world is the landscape or garden, which is designed to create a sense of integration between the visitor and nature, by providing an atmosphere suitable for meditation, a feeling of harmony, oneness with nature, and even timelessness.

The Japanese language is full of references to nature. It even has a special word to describe the sound of cherry blossoms falling. Japanese flower-arranging is meant to embody principles of reverence and simplicity: one composes the flowers as they should be; then removes half of them, then half of what remain.

For the Japanese, as for Asian cultures generally, religion is more a way of walking or living than a matter of belief or acceptance of someone's teaching. If a Japanese person thinks about religion, she thinks about peace of mind or serenity of spirit rather than a belief in God, a doctrine, or the decrees of Allah or the Bible.

Whereas in the West there is a clear division between good and evil, in Japan, like China, it is a matter of yin and yang, which are two complementary life forces; difficult situations are seen in gray tones, rather than in black and white, and conflict resolution is more highly valued than the assertion of one's rights. Evil is not some fatal infection in our nature, but rather a distortion or break in the harmony of nature. Humans are not expected to subdue nature or have dominion over it but to live in cooperation in all ways possible. Shinto is a good example of a living religion where connection with nature is celebrated.

[1]Campbell told this story at a seminar I attended; it is also noted in *The Power of Myth*, his conversation with Bill Moyers.

[2]The word, "Aikido" is made up of three characters. They mean: (1) harmony (peace, love), (2) the spirit or energy of the Universe, and (3) the way or path—thus: a way of getting into harmony with life-energy. Its founder,

Morihei Ueshiba (1883-1969), was a master of several martial arts who delved deeply into both Zen Buddhism and Shinto and came to realize that true self-defense is not winning over others but winning over the discord within oneself. He was a very close observer of nature and spent many hours in meditation on nature's ways. Here are a few of my favorite quotations from Ueshiba O'sensei (O'Sensei meaning here the ultimate teacher):

"There is evil and disorder in the world because people have forgotten that all things emanate from one source. Return to that source and leave behind all self-centered thoughts, petty desires and anger. Those who are possessed by nothing possess everything."

"[We] must protect the domain of Mother Nature, the divine reflection of creation, and keep it lovely and fresh."

"To injure an opponent is to injure yourself. To control aggression without inflicting injury is the Art of Peace."

"The divine is not something high above us. It is in heaven, it is in earth, it is inside us. Each of us is a miniature universe, a living shrine."

"Life is growth. If we stop growing, we are as good as dead. The Art of Peace is a celebration of the bonding of heaven, earth and humankind."

Chapter Two

Eastern Religions

Hinduism: Enough To Make One Wonder

The most complex of the great religions, Hinduism, focuses on "internal" issues.

"The same stream of life that runs through my veins night and day runs through the world and dances in rhythmic measures." ~*Rabindranath Tagore*

As it is the oldest, Hinduism is also the most complex of the major religions. Hinduism has no Founder, no definite dogma, no one sacred book, no history of reformation to impose restrictions on its thoughts and practices. Its history is one of many layers of development, with practically no weeding out. So Hinduism has many faces. To some, it appears as an extrovert religion of much spectacle, abundant mythology, many gods and superstitious practices. To others, it is profoundly interior, a personal path of spiritual progress, a quest for liberation, even a lifetime of renunciation.

Huston Smith taught that truth is embedded in nature for the West and embedded in society for the Chinese—and for the philosophers of India, it is something internal, an aspect of mind.[1] For the Indian theologian, nature is ungovernable and, in some strange way, unreal, shadowy, ever-shifting and mysterious, and it is useless to try to determine its laws. It's all Maya (magic), a trick, the play of a mysterious cosmic illusion. Unlike China, India could not focus successfully on society because India found itself facing the devilish social problem of a color barrier. Even today the division between the light-skinned Aryan and darker-skinned Dravidian is troublesome. The caste system was invented to break the curse, but, instead, was turned into a device for perpetuating social separation. Having abandoned hope of solving life's problem on a social plane, India turned inward, reasoning that, if only we could understand who we truly are, we might win an inner freedom beyond the oppositions and dilemmas that both nature and society present.

During the 5th and 4th centuries, B.C.E.—the time of the Old Testament prophets when Hinduism was already an old religion—there appeared new texts, the Upanishads that reveal a special knowledge. These texts explain how the "atman", or individual human soul, is actually identical with Brahman, the universal soul of God. Typical are these few lines from the Katha Upanishads: "The senses turn outward. Accordingly, man looks toward what is without and sees not what is within. [The wise person] shuts his eyes to what is without and beholds the Self." This turning inward is deemed necessary because the senses are false witnesses. The world is not what it appears to be. Yet, behind this surface life, there is a deeper life that knows no death. The truth of life is experienced only by those who turn their gazes inward.

One evidence of this introspective emphasis is the elaborateness of Indian philosophy's psychological vocabulary. Coomaraswamy, while curator of the Oriental Museum in Boston, said that for every psychological term in English, there are four in Greek and forty in Sanskrit. Mrs. Rhys Davids listed 20 Pali words whose subtle distinctions of meaning are obscured by the simple English term "desire."

Huston Smith pointed out several modern insights that were discovered and explored in detail in India over two thousand years ago:

1. the realization that our consciousness includes layers of sub-consciousness that control most of our emotional behavior;

2. in addition to the obvious physical body, there is a "sheath of vital force" —that, while still physical, is more subtle and is invisible (comparable are contemporary discoveries concerning the electrical-magnetic field of the body and brain waves);

3. human temperaments are different and may be categorized;

4. what we see is not a simple mirroring of the external world, but, at least in part, a function or projection of the perceiving organism. We have everything from Kantian philosophy to various learning theories and neuro-psychologies of perception that make the same point. It has only been during the last one hundred years or so that the West has given anywhere near the attention to the workings of the human mind as did the ancient Indian philosophers.

There is an emphasis, in much Hindi writing and practice, on renunciation, stilling the senses, giving up all attachments, not caring what happens. But this negativistic tendency is rejected by many modern Hindus, including Sarvepalli Radhakrishnan. He wrote: "The religious soul does not seek for release from suffering in the present life or a place in paradise in the next life. His prayer, in the words of the Upanishad, is 'Lead me from the unreal to the real, lead me from darkness to light, lead me from death to immortality.' The resurrection is not the rise of the dead from their tombs but the passage from the death of self-absorption to the life of unselfish love" (*The Philosophy of Sarvepalli Radhakrishnan*, Paul Schilpp, ed., 1952).

In Hinduism we may find examples of cold, indifferent people who don't care about anything and think they are spiritually superior for it, but there is also abundant love literature and an emphasis on self-knowledge through service. There is the dualistic, separatist idea that we have to choose between a life of purity and detachment or "wallowing in the senses," but there is also the celebration of a natural love life as part of a complete life.

What can we make of the basic Hindu idea that our souls, our true selves, are identical with God? Genuine Hindu yogis are supposed to be able to merge their selves with the Self of the Universe through meditation—but there are dangers, such as in the case of the meditator who was said to reach such a pitch of self-consciousness that he dared not scratch when he had an itch, for fear he was the flea.

Ralph Waldo Emerson was one of the "transcendentalist" American thinkers who was much influenced by his study of Hinduism. Today there are any number of "new age" pronouncements that offer "discoveries" that amount to no more than unsophisticated versions of the ancient religion of Hinduism.

Hinduism offers many examples of both separation - nature is an illusion; only the Mind is real—and connection: "The same stream of life that runs through the world and dances in rhythmic measures dances in your veins this very moment."

[1]Huston Smith, *Essays on World Religion*, edited by M. Darrol Bryant. New York: Paragon House, 1992.

Buddhism: the Power of Negative Thinking

"Stop grasping/clinging!" is a relevant teaching for North Americans. It can lead us to compassion.

"When the iron bird flies, and horses run on wheels . . . the Dharma will come to the land of the red man." ~*Padmasambhava, 8th century Tibetan Buddhist saint*

Students of Buddhist history tell us that Gautama, the Enlightened One, who lived 500 years before Jesus, founded not just a religion, but an entire worldview, which served as foundation for economic, political, artistic and religious life. Unlike Hinduism, Buddhism spread widely, into China, Japan, Tibet, Korea, Central Asia, Indochina, and even to a lesser extent, the West. But the days of Ashoka, the great peace-making and nature-respecting Buddhist king, are long gone, and today we see mainly the debris of Buddhist civilization. So Buddhist religion is appreciated in the West in terms of its psychology.

Siddhartha Gautama lived first as a prince whose father tried to keep sheltered from the world. The story goes that, one day, the prince left home to discover the world for himself. He saw situations of sickness, cruelty and death that moved him to pity and despair. He resolved to overcome those troublesome feelings by a severe ascetic regimen, involving fasting and much meditation. It nearly killed him. There are different versions of the story of how he went on to achieve awakening. They all end with him sitting under the great Bo tree in an enlightened state. Somehow, he was changed, profoundly.

Written sayings attributed to him first appeared over 400 years after his death. Reading them, we find certain "basic truths" repeatedly emphasized. The earliest tradition has it that these verities involve no theology or philosophy or mythology and that the Enlightened One was quick to say that he didn't know about such things as the gods or an afterlife. What he did know about was suffering, the cause of suffering, and the cure for suffering. That was enough to awaken his hearers' interest.

The essence of Buddhist teaching is embodied in the Four Noble Truths: 1. The world is full of suffering. This may be spelled out in detail, if one is so inclined. 2. The cause of suffering is desire, the passions of the mind, rooted in the needs of the body. 3. If desire can be removed, passion will die out, and suffering will end. 4. This can be accomplished by following the Eight-fold Path: Right-Ideas, Resolution, Speech, Behavior, Vocation, Effort, Mindfulness, and Concentration.

Whereas Hinduism emphasizes a belief in the human self as being identical with the eternal, non-changing divine Self, Gautama and his followers could find no such enduring self, nothing whatsoever that does not change continually, nothing permanent. There have been many philosophical positions defended within Buddhism, but this one dominates: human suffering arises from the inevitable conflict between our belief in or longing for permanence and the impermanence that we actually experience in all that we cling to and hold dear. True happiness, then, may only be found by reaching a state of non-clinging: freedom from the delusion of permanence.

This may be said to be a timely teaching since we have learned through biology that every cell in our bodies (including our brains) is replaced within a few years, and physicists tell us that all matter is nothing but energy in flux. Nothing lasts as it is: it is all changing, every moment.

How did we ever get the idea that "we" exist—that there is any "me" that prevails through all this flux? How may we speak of an enduring self or soul? What holds together the sense of being an ongoing person? Buddhist philosophy centers around the idea that the ever-changing forces of our bodies and minds forms a cycle of continuity that will go on as long as does the desire to be and to become. That desire will only stop when its driving force is cut off. The goal of Buddhist practice is to control your mind in order to cut off desire. That is a good example of what Albert Schweitzer called "life-negating" religion. He noted that the original meaning of the word "Nirvana" is "to blow out," as with a candle. No more flame. Like Schweitzer, I've not been able to think of that as a desirable state.

Buddhism could never have lasted and grown solely by means of that sort of negativity. "Nirvana" may be interpreted in life-affirming terms as we focuses on the attitude of "grasping," clinging—the compulsive nature of much of our living—that we need to let go of, in order to free up more positive energies. Rather than encouraging practices leading to "extinction," the emphasis is on the removal of impediments to a fuller life.

A full life includes the sort of enlightenment that leads

to compassion. The Buddha chose to leave his blissful state and return to the everyday world in order to share his wisdom - doing this out of compassion. Many times we read that the Buddha was "moved to pity," which does not seem to be a feeling-less state. If one is released from a state of clinging, one is free to become selfless - capable of active compassion of someone who has broken through the apparent distinction between "self " and "other." That breakthrough would seem to imply the realization of a sense of connection with others as being a necessary ingredient of compassion.

It may seem ironic that this emphasis on compassion arises in the context of a Buddhist philosophy in which the stated goal is to get rid of ALL desire. After all, "compassion" is a sort of passion. A strong feeling of connection with someone else is a necessary ingredient. How can anyone feel real empathy or sympathy in a purely disinterested way? It must be that the reasonable objective is to temper compassion with careful, respectful, responsible, thoughtful regard for the true well-being of the other person. But to be effective, compassion, empathy or sympathy must be deeply felt; otherwise, we won't have the energy to put it into practice.

The compassionate decision, which we all face every day, is based on the conflict between wanting to reach out or stay safely within, to give of ourselves or hold back, even to give away too much and perhaps not take proper care of ourselves or our loved ones. Getting some control of our acquisitiveness, our need to accumulate more and more (constantly encouraged by those who have something to sell) can go a long way toward developing a capacity for compassionate action.

The Buddhist "power of negative thinking"—emptying out the mental rubble—turns into something positive when it leads us to realize that we have within us a wealth of compassion that waits to be uncovered and released. Clearing the mind, emptying oneself by letting go of impediments such as a desire for things we don't need in order to reach a deeply felt sense of love for other living beings: this is surely the best of Buddhism.

Taoism and Confucianism: Nature and Society

The nature/nurture controversy is nothing new.
Confucianism connects people.
Taoism connects people with nature.

"Something there is whose veiled creation was before the earth or sky began to be. So silent and so alone, it changes not, nor fails, and all life comes from it. It wraps everything with love as in a garment, and yet it claims no honor: it does not demand to be Lord. I do not know its name, and so I call it Tao, 'the Way.' Pressed to explain, I call it outgoing, far-reaching, and returning."
~*From the 25th chapter of the Tao Te Ching, attributed to the legendary Lao Tsu, "wise old one."*

Taoism and Confucianism are two sides of the same religious coin. Chinese people practice both, with some Buddhism included. In other words, nature and civilization are the polarities of their culture, just as with ours, only they have a different attitude toward this problem.

People in the West usually think of religion in terms of belief in a Supreme Being, and so neither Taoism nor Confucianism (nor Buddhism) are considered real religions, but rather are thought to be no more than philosophies. Religion, however, is a way of tying together our beliefs and our practices, and a blending of Taoism and Confucianism is the way Chinese people do it. Chinese religion is humanistic, not in the narrow sense that denies or slights powers beyond us, but in the realization of a unity of humankind with nature with a strong emphasis on the human role in taking responsibility for living according to the Way of Life.

Chinese religion was an outgrowth, not of philosophical or psychological speculation, but of social changes that resulted around the time of the Hebrew King David (1,000 B.C.E.) in the transformation of Chinese society from tribal to feudal. The formation of the Chou dynasty encouraged human ingenuity and ability, cultivated new trade and talents, and encouraged the development of experts from all levels of society. Prayers for rain were replaced by irrigation. A slave became a prime minister. All this set the stage for the formation of an underlying point of view.

By around 500 B.C.E., Confucius taught that the mandate of Heaven was that of a self-existing moral law by which people could become virtuous. A good society could be developed by cultivating "human-heartedness" and the social virtues—first within oneself, then within one's family and then expanding into the community. Sad to say, Confucianists have tended to apply this idea more to men than to women, whom Confucius classified with servants. He was mainly interested in the development of moral standards leading to virtuous public service.

Confucius wanted rulers to develop a personal integrity that would enable them to understand and fulfill the needs of the people and to care for their welfare. It is in this context that Confucius developed his version of the Golden Rule: "Do not do anything to another that you would not want done to you."

Confucius didn't care to discuss spiritual matters like life after death. He believed that it is more important to understand man than nature, much less anything supernatural. His chief concern was a good society based on good government, which rules by moral example, not force or punishment, a government that fosters harmonious relationships. One of his better sayings is: "Leading an uninstructed people to war is to throw them away."

One of the most important Confucian teachers, Mencius, who lived around 300 B.C.E., exemplified Confucianism with the image of a good Emperor encouraging the people in such a way that they "discover for themselves" their own moral nature. He taught that people are good at heart and only need to be encouraged. By contrast, another Confucianist, Hzun Tzu, believed in the human tendency toward evil, so that people need to be held in check by social custom. Our Western "nature/nurture" controversy is nothing new.

Confucius died in 479 B.C.E. when the society he was supposed to make virtuous was falling apart. Lao Tzu composed the *Tao Te Ching* as his remedy: return to the ancient wisdom of the Tao, the Way of Life. Learn how to let things take their natural course. "As for those who would take the whole world to tinker with as they see fit [he meant the Confucianists], I observe that they never succeed: for the world is a sacred vessel not to be altered by man. The tinkerer will spoil it." This attitude is based on the old Chinese principle: "wu wei," which means "not doing." As Lao Tzu put it, "Alive, a person is supple, soft; in death unbending. All creatures, grass and trees, alive are plastic and pliant, and dead are friable and dry. Unbending rigor is the mate of death and yielding softness the company of life. The strong and mighty topple from their place; the soft and yielding rise above them all."

Lao Tzu taught that, since action involves force, every force will meet with a counterforce. It is best to yield, like water. Use force only with sadness. Go to war, if need be, with the attitude that you are going to a funeral. Indeed, there will be many funerals. Cause others to want what you want, not by force or command, but by your example. Leaders should act so that when the work is finished, the people will say, "We've done it ourselves." (Nothing anti-Confucian here.) Yield when possible. Help the other "save face. "To make another feel inferior is to encourage aggressiveness. Look for ways to meet conflict so that the other person won't lose but have a harmonious result. Taoists believe in the inherent worth and dignity of every person.

According to Lao Tzu, the Way of the Universe is not personal, it is indifferent, "not our kind," yet it supports us by its organic ordering, the primary characteristic of which is spontaneous growth—including what some biologists now call "self-replication." The Way is nameless, with little use of allegories to designate its nature. So we look with interest at the few that are offered: "The great Tao flows everywhere . . . All things depend upon it to exist, and it does not abandon them. To its accomplishments it lays no claim. It loves and nourishes all things, but does not lord it over them."

Taoism: getting back in touch with your own inner

nature by following the Way of nature. Confucianism: "human-heartedness," leading to people dealing fairly with one another. This blending offers the best of Chinese religion and a good way for people to live.

Chapter Three

Middle Eastern Religions

Judaism, Christianity and Islam are usually characterized as Western religions despite the fact that they originated in the Middle East and Islam has little influence in the West—although that influence is growing. We who live in the United States of North America must acknowledge our close connection to two of these religions, Judaism and Christianity, whether believers or not, for our culture is very much a product of Biblical thinking, which is monotheistic and, therefore, intolerant and patriarchal.

A Book of Many Religions

As numerous polls have shown, Americans have high levels of confidence in the Bible. So the widespread problem of biblical illiteracy is not just a problem for individuals. It impacts public policy from local school curricula to international politics. It affects attitudes regarding human rights and responsibilities, and it undermines efforts to address public health issues wherever traditional values clash with present need.

The Hebrew and Christian Bible (claimed as inspired also by Muslims) has been called many things: "The Word of God," "a book of religious literature," "an epic of spiritual discovery (or of religious or moral progress)," even "a bunch of fairy tales." It is hard for an open mind to see any sort of spiritual or moral progress in teachings like Mark 4:11-12 ("To you has been given the secret of the kingdom of God, but for those outside, everything is in parables; so that they may indeed see but not perceive, and may indeed hear but not understand; *lest they turn again, and be forgiven.*") and Revelation 22:10 (". . . for the time is near. Let the evildoer still do evil, and the filthy still be filthy . . .). All of these things cannot be true; but there is some truth to most of them—except that there are no fairy tales in the Bible, and the Bible is not a unified book. It is a collection of 66 books (in the Protestant version), written down over a period of about a thousand years by many more than 66 authors, the identity of most being unknown, despite claims to the contrary. These authors upheld many different, even opposing, points of view.

Although the Bible is the most read, taught and preached book in the world (with the Koran gaining ground), it is also one of the least well understood. A great deal of what is still often said and written about the Bible is not true, or, at best, only partially true. The Bible can't possibly be "The Word of God" (assumed to be self-consistent) because there are many contradictions therein. For examples, John 3:22 and 4:2 have Jesus both baptizing and not baptizing, and Genesis 4:26 and Exodus 6:2 disagree concerning the introduction of the Hebrew name of Yaweh (translated in English as LORD). In Genesis, Yaweh is known at the time of Enosh, a grandson of Adam. In Exodus he is first encountered by Moses.

Despite its wide range of spiritual and ethical

viewpoints, the Bible became the most influential "founding document" of our culture. It is not possible to be well-educated in our culture without having studied the Bible. Yet most people still read into the Bible what they want to find there, rely on passages that seem to support their view, and ignore or misinterpret those that contradict it.

The Bible has been misused to support everything from slavery to a ban against alcohol and an absolute ban on abortion, despite the fact that there is nothing in the Bible to support those positions. These days, a frequent topic is condemnation of homosexuality, based on a very few passages in Leviticus and Paul, despite the fact that Jesus himself nowhere condemned, and even appears to have been tolerant of same-sex relationships. The first part of Luke 7 refers to a Roman centurion's servant "boy," of whom he was "very fond," a common condition with the Roman military. Jesus praised the centurion regarding his faith and offered no condemnation of his sexual preference.

A primary problem of Biblical interpretation is that of translation, the books of the Bible having been written in Hebrew and Greek. There is no such thing as a correct translation of the "divinely inspired word of God," especially of the Hebrew. The very first sentence of the Bible was for centuries translated incorrectly and, therefore, misinterpreted. "In the beginning . . ." is still often said to mean that God created the universe out of nothing at the beginning of time. The Hebrew authors of Genesis had no such idea in mind. A more accurate translation is: "When God began to create, . . ." As we have seen, that work was a re-fashioning of a previously existing creation.

People who try to understand the Bible by memorizing passages in the conviction that the Holy Spirit is leading them to correct interpretation are sadly misguided. There are many statements in the Bible that will never be understood in more than probable terms, as the scholar, Morton Smith, has said. Pious people should learn how to live gracefully with that fact. As another scholar Roland Wolfe pointed out, the Bible is a book of **many** religions—nine, by his reckoning—ranging all the way from the polytheistic mythologies of the first book to the sadism of a vengeful judgment celebrated in the last.

Pharisaic Judaism

Normative Judaism represents the triumph of history over nature.

The religions I have mentioned up to this section all have a character of timelessness. They are more concerned with the places (including that within the individual) *where* the divine may be experienced than with the question, *when* did the divine manifest itself? It was the religion of Judaism that gave humans a sense of history. Judaism centers around events in time: the Exodus from Egypt, the conquest of Palestine, and the development of Jewish culture on that basis. For such events to occur, it was necessary that an ongoing community be formed, having a strong sense of social identity. This was done in terms of a relationship to a god who would (eventually) not be subjected to the limitations to which other gods were subjected, although still limited by the terms of the Covenant. The development of the concept of the god Yaweh (LORD) in the Old Testament, from a local mountain god to the one-and-only supreme ruler of the Universe, took nearly a thousand years.

Moses was not a monotheist. "Thou shalt not have other gods before me" implies the existence of other gods. But, gradually, Yaweh took charge and the other gods—and, of course, the goddesses—fell by the wayside. The Hebrew Bible includes no myth of the origin or nature of God himself. He is simply discovered—or makes himself known - on the mountain and then acts in human history, as it is then said he had been doing all along under different names. His true identity remains mysterious and, therefore, not subject to manipulation (this is the meaning of "You shall not take my name in vain") for the true name is never given, only a riddle: "YHVH" means "I will be who I will be." We find in Judaism none of the life-death-resurrection myths common to other religions of the time—based, as they were, on humanity's relationship with nature, chiefly with the plant world.

Though it has seasonal celebrations, Judaism is not a nature religion. Rather, it is based on events associated with a nomadic people. At its heart lies the Covenant, the promise, an agreement between the representatives of the people and their god. The general idea is: "Obey and all will go well with you." So when things don't go well, it is assumed the people haven't done as commanded. The signs of the covenant are both personal and universal, circumcision and rainbow. The concept gradually gets transformed by the prophets into the ethics of social justice, where God comes to desire—not ritual sacrifice—but good treatment of the weak and vulnerable.

"Remember the Covenant" and "Next year in Jerusalem" are the two key cries of Judaism. They speak of the two foundations of historical religion: memory and hope—and, therefore, of the sense, which Judaism initiated, that all life is caught up in a history, with a beginning, middle, and end.

The concept of God's covenant with his "chosen" people led to intolerance of other beliefs and even persecution of those "others" who held onto them, but it also promoted a sense of shared responsibility, beautifully illustrated by a passage in Exodus where, after the people had again gone after other gods, Yaweh proposed to Moses that He would kill them off and start over. Responding, Moses pleads for the people and says: "If you will not help me save them from their folly, then blot me out of your book!" God Himself is reminded that the Covenant is a two-way agreement that "He who chose Israel" cannot again discard his people as He did in the time of Noah. A higher standard is now required, and so, the people's representative prefers to die rather than go along with a capricious or fickle God. And God changes his mind!—as He does many times in the Bible. Such conversations between God and man represent a process of "humanizing God" where, over time, God becomes more caring and merciful.

What is perhaps most impressive about the religion of the Jews is the belief that the God of the Universe, who is not subject to conditions and cannot be limited in any way, chose to establish a direct relationship with humankind and enter into an historical agreement. This implies that human life is not merely a part of some divine drama wherein we are really nothing but spectators or puppets, and that the Unapproachable chose to get Himself involved with us, even to the point of subjecting His own will to possibilities of human choice—in other words the real freedom of decision-making.

There are further implications of the idea that God entered history and established a relationship with a group of people. We need not discuss the absurd idea that God would choose any one group over others; that is beside the point here—although we cannot afford to forget that it lies at the foundation of much Jewish, Christian and Muslim mischief. The positive side is, if human history is worth divine intervention, then history is real, and therefore, our actions have a lasting effect. Judaism deserves credit for this concept.

Offering no escape from the reality of history, Judaism provides no doctrine of personal immortality. (The idea of a physical resurrection developed late in Old Testament times and has never been held by a majority of Jews.) Responsibility for one's life and the ongoing life of the community is a strong emphasis in Judaism. Learning the history of one's people and passing it on in written form and repeating it in ritual observance according to the written word and educating for progress so as not to repeat the mistakes of the past: all these Jewish ideas have had a profound influence on Western culture.

Although there is frequent disobedience in the Hebrew scriptures, there is almost no notion of original sin in Judaism. The important exception will be mentioned in the section on the development of Christianity out of Essene Judaism. Rather, if people disobey or sin, they're still worth saving, and if the people go astray, they are still worth God's sending another prophet to remind them of their responsibilities. "Go and sin no more" are the words of Jesus the Jew.

According to the Torah, we humans are made out of earth, but still made in God's image. That's quite a combination. It makes Judaism both a very earthy religion and one that can make earthly things radiate with divine light. The modern Jewish philosophical theologian Martin Buber summed up this idea with the expression "hallow all things"—live a natural life as a divine celebration, rather than set religion apart from the rest of life.

I entitled this section *Pharisaic Judaism* because the

Hebrew Bible, as we have it, represents the triumph of that one, in particular, of several branches of the Hebrew religion. Christianity represents—to a much larger degree than is usually understood—the success of the other most significant branch: Essene Judaism.

Essene Judaism

A very un-natural approach to religion that had a much greater influence on Christianity than is generally recognized.

It has been 89 years since the discovery of the Essene Dead Sea Scrolls, and yet their contents are still barely, if at all, known by any but a few thousand readers of books on the subject. This means that most Christians claim belief in something that they cannot possibly understand very well since it is now clear to any discerning Scroll student that understanding much of the New Testament depends, in part, on knowledge of the Dead Sea Scrolls.

The meaning of "Essene" is obscure. The word does not appear anywhere in the Scrolls. There is no known Hebrew or Aramaic reference. It appears only in Greek, and as a designation by outsiders. I believe it comes from a Hebrew word meaning "shunned," but that's another story. The Essenes were a group of Jews who were separated from the Temple priesthood during the first part of the first century B.C.E. and who fled with their Teacher of Righteousness into the desert. After their Teacher was captured and killed, about a hundred of them set up a headquarters ("Qumran") on the Northwest shore of the Dead Sea and lived there until 68 C.E. when the building was destroyed by the Romans.

The latest book of the Hebrew Bible is Daniel (150 B.C.E.). The earliest Christian gospel, Mark, is usually dated 68 C.E., and the earliest rabbinic text, the Mishnah, is usually dated at 200 C.E. The Dead Sea Scrolls, written between 250 B.C.E. and 68 C.E. make up an extensive library of important material during the period in-between. It is "marginal" material, according to Pharisaic Judaism, but its influence on Christianity is enormous. For example, the Essene calendar is solar, as opposed to the normative Jewish lunar calendar, and the Essene Sabbath was not on Saturday but on Sunday—which became the Christian Sabbath.

It is important to note that, contrary to common opinion, the Essene movement was by no means confined to a monastery, but was widespread in the region—estimated at over 4000 followers—having "settled in large numbers in every town," according to the Jewish historian Josephus who wrote that he lived with them for a while. The Roman called Pliny wrote that they "lived in many cities and villages." The "Essene Gate" in Jerusalem has been identified. Now called "Mount Zion," it is on the Eastern side, facing Qumran, and is the entrance to a section of the city that scholars call "the Essene quarter." It is believed to be the site of Jesus' "Last Supper." To what extent that meal was a carry-over from the Essene Messianic banquet is anybody's guess. According to some scholars, it was celebrated according to the Essene solar calendar, rather than the Pharisaic lunar calendar. When a man asked for directions to that event, the third gospel has Jesus telling him to look for a man carrying a jar of water, "and follow him" (Luke 22:10). In that culture, the only sort of person carrying water would have been a woman, a "homosexual", or an Essene priest preparing for baptism. Remnants of the Essene baptismal basins have been discovered in that location.

The Essene scrolls contain three types of writing:

copies of portions of the books of the Torah, including a complete Isaiah but nothing from Esther; commentaries ("pesher") on those scriptures that promote their unique point of view; and writings entirely of their own (including a Temple Scroll, a War Scroll and a Community Rule or Manual of Discipline) that are most revealing of Essene convictions and practices.

It is clear from their writings that the Essenes were obsessed with issues of purity, both ritual and personal, and that they harbored intense hatred of their enemies. For example, the Community Rule contains many vengeful curses against "the lot of Belial," presumed followers of that devil. There would be no mercy for the wicked. None! Their primary concern was the conflict between "The Sons of Light" (themselves and their angelic allies) and "The Sons of Darkness" (the Jews who remained under the influence of the Temple priests and their "devilish" allies). This dualistic approach would find its way into the Christian "New Covenant"—an Essene designation of their community. This approach prevails today in fundamentalisms and even in the thinking of politicians like President George W. Bush, who said, "You're either with us or against us. You're either evil or you're good. This great nation stands on the side of good."

Though he does not seem to have been a practicing member of their community, John the Baptizer summed up the core of Essene conviction by preaching that the End of Days and Reign of God was coming soon, so you'd better turn from your ways, believe, and be baptized into the Kingdom. That proclamation also summarized the message of Jesus according to the earliest gospel, Mark.

Trinitarian Christianity

Trinitarian Christianity embodies a deep ambivalence regarding guilt and the assurance of salvation. Despite an embedded anti-nature bias, Christianity takes matter seriously.

The persistence of traditional Christian beliefs is confirmed by polls over the last few years. These indicate that a substantial majority of adults in the U.S. population believe that Biblical miracles did happen, including Jesus' resurrection from the dead. Most of our fellow North Americans say that they believe in the existence of Satan, the Devil. About half of the populace believes the Second Coming of Jesus will happen within the next thousand years. And nearly half believe the Antichrist is alive on earth now. Such polls show that liberal Christians who do not share such beliefs are in the minority. So those of us who do not count ourselves as Christians are mistaken if we think Trinitarian Christianity has no relevance to our lives as Americans.

"God so loved the world that he . . ." expressed his love directly to the people of the world? Not according to orthodox Christians. By their view, God seems to have been incapable of that, or too angry. Rather, God's way of loving us was to give his Son to be crucified. That's a strange idea. What human father would think of such a thing? Fathers have sacrificed their sons in order to appease or win the favor of a god, but I know of no case where they have thought of such a sacrifice as an expression of their love of other people.

The essence of Trinitarian Christianity is that, first of all, we are unacceptable in God's sight. God is said to be so disgusted with us that, unless something drastic is done, we will suffer eternal punishment. That's what we deserve, and so we ought to feel terribly guilty for what we've done to deserve it. What have we done? It turns out that, according to Paul and the Trinitarian Christian theologians, it isn't anything we've done. It's something Adam did, that we somehow inherited. It comes to this: we deserve eternal punishment for having been born!

Think about the psychology involved. It is this: if you are guilty, then you must be punished; otherwise, you remain guilty. Only if you are punished may you be forgiven—and then loved without reservation (God is no longer angry with you). In inverse order: to be loved, you must first be forgiven. To be forgiven, you must first be punished—your sin must be "paid for." Only then is your guilt removed. This is what Trinitarian Christianity offers the believer: to be loved, by being forgiven—without being punished. How can this be?

Athanasius, a 4th century theologian (whose arguments against the Unitarian, Arius, were upheld by the Emperor Constantine) insisted that Jesus as the Christ was both fully human and fully God. His argument went like this: *we are full of sin (being born that way) and are thus guilty and deserving of punishment. No one of us is capable of receiving enough punishment to expiate our sin. Only God could ever take that amount of punishment and still survive. Yet we, and not God, must be punished, because we are the guilty ones.* How could that problem ever be solved? *God did it by becoming one of us and taking all our sin and the punishment due us upon Himself. He bore it for us, as only He could do. He could do this because, in Jesus the Christ, He was both fully God and fully man.* Thus the Christian is saved, not by himself, but by God. We are expected to believe all this as a matter of faith.

Having become conscious of guilt, Christians created a means for overcoming it. Through belief in the sacrifice of Christ, a person may become "acceptable," as the theologian Paul Tillich put it. But there is a deep ambivalence within the Christian churches concerning the assurance of salvation. The church's main purpose appears to be to keep its followers forever in a state of uncertainty about their salvation, and, therefore, dependent upon the church. "Am I saved, or not?" is the question for which the church provides only a tentative answer. Whatever assurance is given is qualified with the caveat: one can never know for certain; only God knows.

The belief is that being too convinced of your salvation is prideful, because God, after all, has the right to count you among the damned. "Thy will be done" is therefore the only pious position. Who are you to say what God's will should be? It is best to do as you're told as evidence of your faith. This approach to religion rests on a sad situation: a great many people of Christian culture are not able to accept a belief that "God is love" (1 John 4:8) without tying it in to guilt and punishment (despite John's having written that God's love has nothing to do with punishment). Someone's got to be punished before God can love us.

How can we explain this peculiar fascination with guilt and punishment? Consider that the strongest feeling in us, the sexual urge, is also in our culture (as a rule) deprived of a fully natural and wholesome expression. Pornography we have aplenty, but that's not love. It's exploitation. Guilt about sexuality and the various perversions that result, lie at the root of Western wounded-ness. If you offer someone forgiveness who has no feeling of having sinned, she will fail to see the need for it. (That made for a problem for missionaries who tried to convert Native Americans.) It has been the difficult task of Christian proselytizers to convince people of their sin and guilt in order to make forgiveness a desired necessity.

Christianity tells us that God entered history in a unique, decisive and final way in order to ensure salvation for believers. This means that history has a beginning (Genesis), a middle (Jesus, the Christ) and an end (the Second Coming and final Reign of God). This idea of history provided humankind with a radically new sense of significance: humankind was no longer to participate in the perpetual re-enactment of an archetypal drama. Rather, each person would play her unique part in the once-and-for-all drama of history. Just as God's action was unique, so are each person's. Each of us may then look upon our life as a unique story and on scientific and social achievement as having lasting significance.

Despite a deeply embedded anti-nature bias, Christianity takes *matter* seriously. "God so loved the world" (rather than "the souls of the world") implies the world as lovable. And Christianity has paid matter the highest of compliments with the concept of the incarnation: that God actually became flesh and blood. If God became a material man, then a material man was God, and to that extent matter may be considered of ultimate significance.

In both Pharisaic Jewish and orthodox Christian

tradition—right down to the modern social gospel—the Kingdom of Heaven is supposed to arrive on earth. It is not some otherworldly spiritual state. Even in death, this way of perceiving will not desert the body. If there is to be life after death, it, too, must include the physical: the resurrection of the body. That is the orthodox belief, and we who do not hold to it should still be able to see that it implies something positive about the stuff of which we are made.

It can even imply something positive about nature as a whole. There is a "creation spirituality" element in Christianity that would have all of nature a part of God's Kingdom when salvation is complete. When Creation is severed and the believer insists on man's "fallen" nature, what is there to do but try to find a way to heal the wound and bring it all back together?—so that, once more, God can call it all good. There must be a way to do that.

I'll mention just a few of the many Christian heresies to illustrate the point that, from the beginning, Christianity was divided by different points of view concerning the meaning of salvation. The first may be found in the New Testament itself: the letter attributed to James, Jesus' brother, presumed to be the founder of the earliest Christian church, in Jerusalem. Taking issue with Paul, he writes, "What does it profit, my brethren if a man says he has faith but has not works? Can his faith save him? . . . faith by itself, if it has no (good) works, is dead" (2:14,17). And: "You see a man is justified by works and not by faith alone" (2:24). This contradicts the salvation-by-faith-alone doctrine of Paul that became the norm of Christian theology. The Antioch Christians prevailed over the Jerusalem followers of Jesus.

In the 3rd century, Origen of Alexandria (who was considered a great defender of Christian belief until declared a heretic) held out for universal salvation, not only for all people, but even the devil and all spirits. Only then could God be "all in all." Abelard, a 13th century theologian, offered a humane interpretation of the suffering and death of Jesus by saying that it wasn't a matter of redemption or atonement, but that Jesus was savior (Christ) in the sense that he elected to suffer and die in order to evoke in our hearts a sense of compassion for the suffering of life, to take our minds and hearts beyond commitment to the material goods of the world and turn us in empathy to his example, and, thereby, to have sympathy for others.

Those are only three examples of heretical teachings within Christianity. It has been quite an effort for even the most orthodox theologians to avoid heresy - witness the long struggle to clarify the nature of the Trinity, wherein, one after the other, theologians were killed, banished, or labeled heretics for not "getting it right". Was Christ the created or "adopted" Son of the eternal Father, or the eternal Son of the Father (and thus "of one substance" with Him)? When your life is at stake, it's important to put the adjective in the right place. Such philosophical hair-splitting is now rare, except in the strictest churches; rather, people are told they must simply "accept Jesus as your personal savior"- or else! Even the "or else" part is downplayed in the more liberal churches; but then, what are we being saved from?

Gnostic Christianity

The Gnostic gospels offer an interesting mix of views concerning the human connection to the natural world and to God. Some of their teachings are amazingly New Age.

Whether Christians or not, our lives are influenced every day by Christian culture. But we've been deprived of the extent of that culture by the promoters of orthodoxy (Trinitarian Christianity) who have done what they could to suppress the wide diversity of views held by the earliest Christians. Since the 1940s, some important discoveries have helped to clarify this problem.

In 1945 (near the time of the Dead Sea Scroll discovery), a large body of "Gnostic" (the word means special or spiritual knowledge) works came to light: the *Nag Hammadi Library*, consisting mostly of early Christian writings that had been suppressed by the early church "fathers." Until then, we knew about Gnostic teaching only by means of a few documents and mainly in terms of orthodox fulminations against those heresies.

Some of the Gnostic writings were contemporary with those of the New Testament. As an example, the Gnostic *Gospel of Thomas* is counted by the 75 or so scholars of *The Jesus Seminar* as authentic enough for them to list it as a fifth gospel. The best known of those *Jesus Seminar* scholars, John Dominic Crossan, says that at least the earliest edition of Thomas was composed by sometime in the 50s C.E., earlier than any of the canonical four! That early dating is, however, controversial. A lot hangs on such dating for those interested in the quest for the historical Jesus.

It used to be thought that Gnosticism was a minor, short-lived heresy within early Christianity. Now we know that it included Jewish and Greek, as well as Christian elements, and that Gnostic influences have continued up to the present time. Many traces of that way of thinking remain in the New Testament.

The common view is that the Gnostics believed that, as a result of a primal, catastrophic "splitting," the universe became alienated from God, and that all of nature as we know it was created by an evil force. We are therefore part of a "fallen" nature. All that remains of God is a "spark" or "fragment" that resides somewhere within us, but to which we have no access—without the special knowledge of Gnostic teaching. It may seem, therefore, that Gnosticism represents an extremely "separatist" view, of man versus nature. That may be true regarding much Gnostic teaching, but that judgment appears to be an oversimplification concerning Gnosticism as a whole.

An important aspect of connection with nature is our view of women. Men who use religion as a vehicle to rise above nature usually have a jaundiced view of women as writings of the early church fathers show. At least some of the Gnostic Christians seem to have been more nature-connected in this regard. The orthodox gospels have retained something of their view, by having the resurrected Jesus first appear, not to Peter or any of the male disciples after his death, but to a woman: Mary Magdalene. It is not surprising then, that the Gnostic gospels have more to say about her.

Scholars say that the *Gospel of Mary* was written during sometime in the second century, but the time and places of the earliest circulation of its sayings is anybody's guess. When the disciples were gathered after Jesus was gone for good, this gospel has Peter say to Mary: "Sister, we know that the Savior loved you more than the rest of the women." The *Gospel of Philip* also says that Mary Magdalene was Jesus' "companion" and that he used to "kiss her often on the mouth."

The Gospel of Mary has her telling the men things that only she knew and asserts that Jesus had instructed her regarding the relationship between mind, spirit and soul and other such esoteric concerns. The conflict between the prevailing church fathers and the Gnostic believers is summarized in the *Gospel of Mary* where, as the men argue about the authenticity of her pronouncements, Peter summarizes the men's' view: "Did he really speak with a woman without our knowledge? Are we to turn about and listen to her? Did he prefer her to us?"

Despite their positive view of direct religious experience, the Gnostics, generally, held a gloomy view of the created world—and of the world's creator, whom they regarded as an evil force—and many of them taught the virtue of giving up such things as sex and money for the sake of spiritual achievement. Regarding the resurrection, the four New Testament gospels and Paul's writings present a confusing picture. Was it physical, was it "ghostly," or was it a visionary experience? The Gnostics were united on this point: the risen Christ was a spiritual being who was experienced by means of visions. The important thing was not whether one took the word of a few men who claimed to have seen his risen body (they refused to believe the women and had to have the experience for themselves), but rather actually to experience the risen Christ in one's own mind and heart. Of course, they insisted this is what Jesus himself taught.

The diversity of views within Christian Gnosticism regarding women is evident from their writings. *The Gospel of Thomas* ends with these words: "Simon Peter said to them, 'Let Mary leave us, for women are not worthy of life.' Jesus said, 'I myself shall lead her in order to make her male, so she too may become a living spirit resembling you males. For every woman who will make herself male will enter the kingdom of heaven.'" He was not talking about gender reassignment surgery. A common Gnostic view was that things of the earth are feminine and those of the heavens (origin of spirit) masculine, and so "making her male" meant initiating her into the secrets of the men's spiritual society.

That women often played an equal role with men in the Gnostic communities is shown by the fact that they served as deacons and even bishops who served communion, healed the sick, and prophesied. Church fathers such as Tertullian found this outrageous: "They have no modesty; they are bold enough to teach, to engage in argument, to enact exorcisms, to undertake cures, and, it may be, even to baptize!"

The Gnostic gospels present an interesting mix of views concerning the human connection to the natural world and to God. Whereas the orthodox view was this: "The kingdom of God is **among** or **with** you"—in the person of Jesus, who suffered, died, and physically rose again as true believers will rise at the appointed time—the Gnostic view was the following: "The kingdom of God is

within you" (Matthew's version) in the sense that salvation is not faith in having one's sins forgiven but, rather, the attainment of knowledge of who you really are. The Gnostics held the orthodox view of sin and salvation to be naive, as well as incorrect. They taught that the true God, the true Christ, is to be found in one's own mind, and nowhere else.

Many of their writings have the disciples questioning Jesus concerning the location of the Kingdom of God or time of its appearance. He refuses to respond in those terms or to tie its attainment to any church structure. Rather, as Thomas has it, Jesus says, "The kingdom of the Father is spread out upon the earth, but men do not see it." And "Lift a stone, I am there. Cleave a piece of wood and I am there." Think of what you may see when you split rotten wood or lift up a rock.

According to the Gnostics, self-ignorance is a form of self-destruction; whoever doesn't understand the essentials of a spiritual life is bound for annihilation. So how does one find this special knowledge within oneself? A typical gnostic teaching is, "If you bring forth what is within you, what you bring forth will save you. If you do not bring forth what is within you, what you do not bring forth will destroy you." Has any modern psychologist put it better?

The Gnostics taught that insight comes only through effort: "Recognize what is before your eyes, and what is hidden will be revealed to you." That can be hard to do. Thomas even warns that self-discovery involves inward turmoil: "Jesus said, 'Let him who seeks continue seeking until he finds. When he finds, he will become troubled. When he becomes troubled, he will be astonished, and he will (then) rule over all things.'"

The Gnostic *Dialogue of the Savior* has the disciples asking for the location of "the place of life, the pure light." Jesus answers: "Everyone who has known himself has seen it." And *The Testimony of Truth* says that the true seeker becomes "**A disciple of his own mind**," discovering that his own mind "is a father of the truth." Some of the Gnostics, like the Tibetan Buddhists, even taught that **all** gods are but creations of our own minds!

The *Gospel of Philip* explains that truth can only be conveyed in symbols or metaphors, as with the parables of Jesus because religious language is that of inward transformation, and whoever perceives reality becomes what he sees: "You saw the spirit, you became spirit. You saw Christ: you became Christ. What you see you shall become." So achieving gnosis means, not being a Christian, but becoming Christ! Of course, the Gnostic teachers provided elaborate methods for achieving such knowledge, including various ascetic practices.

When it comes to ethics, they appear to have held a simple view: Thomas has the disciples asking various detailed questions, to which Jesus replies only: "Do not tell lies, and do not do what you hate."

It is not hard to understand why the Trinitarian teaching had a broader appeal. All one had to do was confess Christ as savior, according to their interpretation, obey the bishops, repent and refrain from further sin, witness to the faith—and you're in, forever. The Gnostics offered no such guarantee, claiming only that the truth that people sought was within them.

Any gospel that sees God under a rock can also see God in you and me, and, will try to teach us to see God in one another. To put it another way: it is one Life that lives in all of us, and the word for that life is God. Or, as Joseph Campbell said, "When you see the kingdom spread out upon the earth, the old way of living in the world is annihilated. ***That*** is 'the end of the world' . . . (and then) you see, not the world of solid things, but a world of radiance"[1] —that was there all the time.

Is the Gnostic view anti-natural? It depends on how we view the "Kingdom of God." What if the Kingdom of God is not something that comes into the world from without, but something that "infuses" everything like a sort of divine perfume?

---

[1] Joseph Campbell, *The Power of Myth (with Bill Moyers)*. New York: Doubleday, 1988.

Zoroaster, Angels and Essene Christianity

Zoro did return, in Christianity and Islam, with his dualistic inventions of good and evil forces, heaven and hell, and the resurrection of the body. "Angelification" is a denial of oneself as a part of nature. Ernest Renan (1863) was right: "Christianity is an Essenism that has largely succeeded."

We are familiar with the Christian drama of a cosmic battle between God and the Devil, with Satan's expulsion from heaven and his perverse influence upon the lives of men. That fantasy was fleshed out by the Englishman, John Milton, in his *Paradise Lost*. The theme of victory over the Devil and all the dark forces of evil, a victory brought about by the Messiah, Son of God, head of the forces of Light and Truth, runs through the New Testament—as it does the Essene Dead Sea Scrolls.

Before the discovery of the Dead Sea Scrolls, scholars assumed that the authors of the Christian New Covenant must have been highly influenced by Zoroastrianism and Platonic philosophy. That was so, to some extent, but we know now that we don't need to look so far afield for doctrines that were formulated and taught at Qumran and in the Essene enclaves. We may still ask: Where did the Essenes get their dualistic view of things? Was it just a development of Old Testament concepts, or was there a Zoroastrian influence?

The Iranian prophet Zoroaster is thought to have lived sometime between the 16th and 6th centuries B.C.E.—a huge discrepancy! In any case, his religion was well-founded by the time of the late books of the Old Testament and those that followed. Zoroaster began his career as a priest of the ancient Iranian religion of the Magi. "Magi" are magicians. Some are mentioned in the New Testament, including, of course, Jesus. (See *Jesus the Magician*, by Morton Smith.) Zoroaster reformed the religion he inherited, and Zoroastrianism became the faith of the Persian Empire through the mid-seventh century C.E., when the Muslims drove it out. Today, there are only about a hundred thousand or so Zoroastrians, called "Parsis," in India, and a few thousand, at most, in Iraq.

A major religion has mostly vanished, except to the extent that Judaism, Christianity and Islam retain what they gained as a result of Zoroastrian influence. Zoroastrians and Jews lived amicably, side by side, throughout the Hellenistic world, being bound together by their mutual grievances against Greek and Roman rule. The last book of the Hebrew Bible, Daniel, and the inter-testament works (such as the very influential books of Enoch) were written in the context of that political provocation. We find in Daniel, in inter-testament books like Enoch and the Dead Sea Scrolls, and also in the Christian New Covenant, and in the Koran, ideas that were, at most, only hinted at by the authors of the Hebrew Bible.

Zoroaster saw the world in polarized terms. His god had an evil twin, who was lord of death and destruction. The ceaseless war between the twin gods would end some day with the triumph of the good one. All human conflict was set into that context. Evidently, Zoroaster believed (as would the Essenes and Jesus) that the triumph of good over evil would occur in his own lifetime. Since this did not happen, he had the foresight to envision a future messianic figure, who would eventually prevail over the forces of darkness and resurrect the dead. Zoroaster promoted the idea of the resurrection of the dead. Before him, most people in the Middle East, including the writers of the Old Testament, believed that the dead would descend to a dreary condition underground (Sheol, in Hebrew), except for the few favored by the gods. In Zoroaster's vision, all believers went to the skies and their opponents to an underground place of punishment. So he added Heaven and Hell to his many inventions, and also the image of the resurrection of the body, which would be transformed by a divine fire—which explains the fire worship of the Zoroastrians.

An obsession with the end of the world still provides a theological basis for today's terrorism. Both Christian and Islamic fundamentalist leaders preach looming cataclysms inspired by ancient writings. When you believe that the end is near and that your actions will hasten this "rapture," every atrocity leading to that end is sanctioned. It is disquieting to note that, as their government prepared them for a second war against Iraq, those Americans who considered themselves religious were more in favor of going to war than those who opposed that action at that time.

The Hebrew Bible, including Daniel, knew nothing of an evil principle, independent of God. Satan, in the book of Job, is an authorized accuser, sanctioned by Yaweh. He could not operate of his own will. It is in the time of the non-canonical books of the inter-testament period that Satan (the Essene's favorite term was "Belial") began his career as a rebel against God. Some of the Essene commentators, all writing before New Testament times, seem to have enjoyed elaborating on the life of the devil.

The Essene writings make it clear that they hated those remaining in charge of the temple in Jerusalem, believing them and their followers to be under the control of Belial. The ruling group included the great Hillel, a primary founder of Pharisaic Judaism. The Essenes called the Temple priests Sons of Darkness, as the Essenes were the Sons of Light. This is one of many Essene terms that found its way into the Christian New Covenant ("... that you may become Sons of Light"—John 12:36). Other examples are "the Poor" and "the Many," "followers of the Way," and "Nazarenes," all of which are meant to refer to members of the sect itself. John the Baptizer almost certainly had an Essene background, and most of the New Testament writers were at least a little influenced by the Essene point of view.

Belief in angels, special sorts of dreams, near-death experiences, visions of beings of light, and apocalyptic expectations—all tied into the hope for personal resurrection or immortality: these are widespread in our culture. Polls show that most Americans believe in angels of one sort or another. All of these beliefs represent an attempt to go beyond nature.

Our Mormons, Adventists, Pentecostals and other indigenous faiths focus on end-time visions, which may seem unique to their particular religions, despite the fact that such visions are nothing new. What is missing is knowledge—of the long ancestry of such beliefs, as they arose in human history and were then elaborated upon—an understanding of the ways by which such beliefs entered into Judaism and Christianity and Islam and became embedded.

Angels rarely appear in the Hebrew Bible, and when they do, they are mere messengers from God—until the book of Daniel, written about 165 years before Jesus. The angelology of Daniel is more Zoroastrian than Jewish. The angels begin to be named and, for the first time, prophesy the future, by interpreting Daniel's dreams. Michael and Gabriel, guardian angels of Israel, are the first of what Harold Bloom called "an angelic avalanche that comes down upon the people of God" in the apocalyptic literature of roughly 200 B.C.E. through 200 C.E.[1]

The central image of Zoroaster's vision was a cleansing fire. In Judaism, a heavenly fire transformed Enoch—a mysterious patriarch of whom we are told (in Genesis) only that he "walked with God, and then was not, because God took him"—into Metatron, greatest of angels, who became crucial in non-Biblical, but influential Jewish mystical teaching. The image of an astral body of light goes back at least to the India of the Vedas and has even earlier manifestations in Egypt and in shamanism throughout the world. The image is that of ". . . a primordial person, at once both male and female, earlier than Adam or Eve, unfallen and divine, angelic, yet higher than the angels, a vision that blazes with a fiery light" (Harold Bloom, p. 8-9).

One variety of first-century escapism (denial of oneself as a part of nature) is illustrated by a recently translated Dead Sea Scroll fragment, which is part of a text dealing with the process of "angelification," a personal transformation whereby resurrected believers are changed into angels who then take their places in heaven—the common belief being that the stars are angelic beings, "Sons of God." Such a transformation is reserved only for "those in the know," or, to use words attributed to Jesus, those to whom "the mystery of the kingdom of God" has been revealed.

The idea (floated for a while) that the founder of the Essene community, their "Teacher of Righteousness," was a forerunner of Jesus, has been shown to be a misunderstanding. But the Essene Messiah is another matter. First of all, the scholar, Israel Knohl makes an excellent case for the actual historicity of such a figure: "This earlier Messiah described himself as sitting on a heavenly throne surrounded by angels. He regarded himself as the 'suffering servant' who brought in a new age, an age of redemption and absolution in which there was no sin or guilt. These audacious ideas led to his rejection and excommunication by the Pharisee sages under the leadership of Hillel. The Messiah was finally killed in Jerusalem, and his body was left in the street for three days. His disciples believed that he had arisen after three days and had ascended to heaven."[2] Knohl identified this Messiah as the Essene, Menachem, who was Hillel's main rival, and who, with his followers, was kicked out of the Temple when his radical and self-serving view became known.

Why all this concern about a Messiah? Because, as Knohl emphasized, that Messiah ". . . would bring them atonement for their sins." This messianic "suffering servant" who "atones for their iniquity" (as the scroll itself puts it) was, therefore, not an invention of Christianity as has been generally assumed but was well established in the Essene community. "This messianic interpretation of Isaiah 53 was *not* discovered in the Christian Church. It had already been developed by the Messiah of Qumran."

One of the many beliefs shared by the Essenes and some of the early Christians was their notion of the cause and effect of man's deplorable condition: sin and predestination. The Hebrew scripture, though it speaks of sin, does not contain a doctrine of original sin: a universal inclination to do evil, an evil nature. It is still commonly thought that this notion was a Christian invention. What, then, are we to make of such Essene phrases as "Can flesh born of the guilty inclination be glorious?" and reference to man's "inclination to sin and the sorrow of transgression?"

This Essene concern with an inborn sinful inclination ties in well with their doctrine of predestination, which is founded on a notion of two spirits: "For in accordance with the everlasting Spirits (of good and evil) Thou hast cast a lot for all the sons of men between goodness and ungodliness and hast sealed their reward." And "Thou hast ordained the way of every man together with his visitation before ever creating him."

The Essene doctrine of two everlasting spirits, the Spirit of Truth (Prince of Light, Angel of Truth) and the Spirit of Wickedness (Perversity, Prince of Darkness, Satan, Belial), had those spirits living together within everyone, being engaged in a constant struggle for men's souls. But the final outcome was determined by God who "ordained the way of every man" and "sealed their reward." "Before they were created, he knew their deeds. He knew all the things that have happened and the things that would happen forever."

One of the earliest scroll scholars, A. Dupont-Sommer, wrote in 1962: "The documents from Qumran make it plain that the primitive Christian Church was rooted in the Jewish sect of the New Covenant, the Essene sect to a degree none of us would have suspected and that it borrowed from it a large part of its organization, rites, doctrines, 'patterns of thought' and its mystical and ethical ideas."[3] His translator, Geza Vermes, a cautious and very respectable scholar who has written much about the scrolls, includes that quotation in the last chapter of his 1999 book, *An Introduction to the Complete Dead Sea Scrolls*, wherein he tries to soften Dupont-Sommer's judgment, without actually contradicting it.

Vermes was mistaken, however, in asserting that ". . . there is no reason whatever to suppose that Jesus, in Galilee, ever encountered any Essenes." According to Matthew 5:43f, Jesus said, "You have heard it said, you shall love your neighbor and hate your enemy. But I say to you, Love your enemies, . . ." There is no such saying as that to which he refers in the Hebrew Bible. But the Essene Community Rule has those entering their New Covenant taking a binding oath, swearing forever to "love all the Sons of Light, hate all the Sons of Darkness, love all that He has chosen and hate all that He has rejected." Jesus spoke specifically against that Essene point of view.

Considering the extent of Essene Judaism and also the location of Jesus' baptism and much of his ministry, he must have known a lot about their beliefs and practices and may even have joined them for a while. But by the time of his ministry, and with John dead, he was on his own. Unlike the Essenes, he made a point of associating with "unclean" people (lepers and prostitutes, and so on) and breaking various ritual, dietary and social rules that would have offended them deeply and, according to the gospels, did offend the Sadducees and Pharisees. Also, Luke 16 has Jesus casting the "Sons of Light" in an unfavorable manner. Jesus cannot be put into the mold of any contemporary group, other than Judaism in general.

The 19th century French New Testament Scholar, Ernest Renan, was prescient indeed when (well before the discovery of the Dead Sea Scrolls) he wrote that "Christianity is an Essenism that has largely succeeded."[4] That success took much of humanity further away from our natural connection than perhaps any other development in the history of religion.

[1] Harold Bloom, *Omens of Millennium*. NY: Riverbend Books, 1996, p. 8.
[2] Israel Knohl, *The Messiah Before Jesus: The Suffering Servant of the Dead Sea Scrolls*. Berkeley: University of California Press, 2000.
[3] Dupont-Sommer, *The Essene Writings from Qumran*. Cleveland: Meridian Books, 1962.
[4] Ernest Renan, *Life of Jesus*, 1863.

Islam's Way of Submission

As with Judaism and Christianity, the gulf between the moderates and the fundamentalists in Islam is much wider than between Islam and the other religions.

In 1978 in an article in the *National Geographic*, the director of the United States Islamic Center wrote in glowing terms of the once-in-a-lifetime experience that many Muslims have during their pilgrimage to their holy city, Mecca—something Muslims have been doing for thirteen centuries. He summed up his view of the role of religion in his life: "The joy of Islam lies in its recognition and fulfillment of man's various needs. Unburdened by and innocent of the sin of any other, we are encouraged to pursue our material, emotional and intellectual urges and are rewarded by God for fulfilling them." He went on to speak of the importance of remembering our origins in the Creator to whom we return at death and of the ritual obligations called the Five Pillars of Islam: belief, prayer, almsgiving, fasting and pilgrimage.

With about a billion followers, Islam is second only to Christianity in numerical strength and is the fastest growing religion in the world. Its founder, Mohammed, lived in the early part of the 7th century, C.E. Orphaned as a child, he was brought up by relatives and received little education. As a young man, he went to work for a wealthy widow who was much older than he was. He was to marry her and carry out several successful trading missions for her where he learned much about Christianity and Judaism. He also learned fasting and vigils as techniques for producing—in persons of his temperament—mind-boggling experiences not unlike those yielded in our day by LSD or peyote. He spent much time in meditation in a cave outside Mecca and there underwent a transformation wherein, it is said, the angel Gabriel dictated the verses of the Koran, which Islam regards as God's eternal and infallible Word.

Mohammed had to flee from those who weren't ready to accept his new teaching, but within ten years, all of Arabia was under his sway, and within 125 years of his death, Islam had taken over most of the Mediterranean world. Islam now dominates the Middle East, most of Africa and Indonesia, and is making inroads in other parts of the world.

Perhaps the most important factor in the incredibly fast spread of Islam is its simple straightforwardness. "Islam" means submission or surrender to the will of Allah, in whose eyes all are equal, and in whose service, all are brothers and sisters. Islam represents an advance over what preceded it. For example, the social status of women was greatly improved. Koranic law guarantees the right of a woman to divorce, to own property, and to inheritance. But, despite these guarantees, many Muslim women are still forbidden to work outside the home, denied political rights such as a fair trial, or live in fear of abuse by the men in their lives.

The Koran says that individual freedom of belief, speech, travel, work and education, are sacred rights to be guaranteed and defended by the government, which, of course, is to be based on the Koran. There is no separation of church and state in Islam. Islam at its best is pledged to developing a society of equal opportunity for all, rooting out corruption, exploitation and all practices that would provide an unfair advantage for one segment of society over the rest.

Would that one could leave it at that; however, recent experience of Islam, as practiced by the fundamentalist regimes of Afghanistan, Iran, Saudi Arabia, and elsewhere, presents us with a very different view of that religion. We see radical mullahs exhorting their followers to a jihad (Muslims would remind us of another meaning of jihad in addition to "the fight against enemies of Islam". The word also means the spiritual struggle within oneself against sin). We also see Islamic spiritual leaders issuing violent fatwas, organized terrorists united and motivated by Islamic identity, state-sanctioned Islamic schools indoctrinating young men in violent anti-Western rhetoric, and appalling punishments dictated by criminal codes based on Islamic law.

In her book, *Nine Parts of Desire: The Hidden World of Islamic Women*, Geraldine Brooks wrote of the progressive Muslims' tendency to blame colonial history, Bedouin tradition, and other pre-Islamic cultures for practices such as female genital mutilation and the stoning of adulterous women. "Yet when the Koran sanctions wife-beating and the execution of apostates, it can't be entirely exonerated for an epidemic of wife slayings and death sentences on authors . . . At some point every religion, especially one that purports to encompass a complete way of life and system of government, has to be called to account for the kind of life it offers the people in the lands where it predominates. It becomes insufficient to look at Islam on paper, or Islam in history, and dwell on the inarguable improvements it brought to women's lives in the seventh century. Today, the much more urgent and relevant task is to examine the way the faith has proved to be such fertile ground for almost every anti-women custom it encountered in the great march out of Arabia."[1]

An American commentator has summed up a common Western impression of present-day Islam by suggesting that, of the major religions, "Islam seems particularly prone to violent interpretations." He mentioned Harvard political scientist, Samuel Huntington's *The Clash of Civilizations*, which offers specific evidences of "militant proclivities" in the Muslim world, and he declared that ". . . as an absolutist faith that mingles religion and politics, Islam is less amenable to the easier co-existence of other creeds . . . and Islam's youth boom, combined with economically stagnant societies, has left a legacy of alienation that aids and abets fundamentalism."[2]

Apparently, Muslims have learned something from Zoroastrianism as well as Essene Christianity with respect to the "us-against-them" attitude. A perpetual state of "holy war" (Sons of Light verses Sons of Darkness) is promoted by fundamentalist Islamic belief. The terrorist organization, Al Qaeda, is led by men who hold fast to an apocalyptic worldview, which is now widely accepted in much of the Muslim world. Their intellectual hero is a philosopher named Sayyid Qutb, whose view of the present human crisis is based, as is mine, on a perception of our loss of contact with human nature. But his perception is a very different one from the one I am upholding. Qutb saw human degeneration, especially in the sexual area, as due to the perversion of Islam by Jews,

Christians, and compromising Muslims. He saw the conflict between Islam and the West as, in essence, one of ideology. He insisted that religion is the issue, and the solution is the reinstatement of shariah, the Muslim code, as the legal code for all of society.

That conviction seems promising to many Muslims, who hold that, with the abolition of man-made laws, no one will be forced to obey mere mortals. Rather, human dignity will be restored by replacing all such false doctrines with God's law—as interpreted by the Muslim theocrats, of course. Paul Berman spelled out this ominous message in an article, "The Philosopher of Islamic Terror," in the *New York Times Magazine* (March 23, 2003), adapted from his book, *Terror and Liberalism*.

Of course, many modern Muslims don't hold such a strict view, and there are similar incentives to violence in other religions. The history of Christianity runs red with blood. But present-day Christian fundamentalism is usually held in check by the majority, who do not hold fast to literal interpretations.

At its best, Islam is a religion of connection. Muslims are taught to reject the old myth of estrangement and the doctrine of original sin and, instead, celebrate humanity's place in the natural world. However, with Islam, as with monotheistic religions generally, God is conceived as a being separate from nature, and our relationship to Him is said to be one of submission, rather than cooperation.

When faith is practiced in terms of submission, it is always a question of who interprets God's will. No wonder the ironic polarities of the monotheistic religions and the "us-against-them" mentality. Divergent interpretations reflect the differing personal agendas of the interpreters.

[1] Geraldine Brooks, *Nine Parts of Desire: The Hidden World of Islamic Women.* NY: Random House, 1995, p. 231.
[2] Scot Lehigh, *Boston Globe*, 3/6/02.

PART III

HUMAN NATURE

In this part of the book, I bring together some old and new insights concerning human nature and the human relationship with the world. After highlighting the issue of objectification, I stress the importance of *feeling* in human nature—and in nature as a whole. This is a crucial concept for the view I am upholding. My third chapter ends with a suggestion concerning the possibility of an energy field functioning as a carrier for thought and feeling. That issue will be addressed more comprehensively in Part IV. Chapter Four of this part, on religion and sexuality presents a view that is compatible with a natural religion. The last chapter offers some reasons for optimism concerning the human role in earth evolution.

Chapter One

The Problem of Objectification

Western religion and philosophy combine with the structure of our language to turn subjects into objects and sever our sense of connection with nature.

Before Biblical beliefs were advanced, the prevailing cosmological myth of humankind upheld the notion that the world exists to nurture us and is not there to be challenged or re-fashioned—much less subdued and dominated. The religions of India, China, Japan and the Americas never seriously questioned this belief, but the religious philosophy of the Middle East— Biblical and Greek philosophy—took issue with it and eventually replaced it with a very different concept.

The Hebrew god was not a nature god, even though the story has him confronting Moses in terms of a volcanic eruption—a telling metaphor for the stupendous revolution in thought that was being initiated. After the exile of the Jews into Babylonia, the Jewish philosophers came to envision Yaweh as creator of the entire natural world. Originally, he had been set apart, separate from "foreign" Canaanite nature-deities. Instead of being fused with nature, as they were, Yaweh was a lord of events, deeds, and what came to be called history.

The Hebrews were nomads, whose god—like them—

was "on the move." The followers of Yaweh moved into the goddess-worshipping, nature-oriented culture and cut it to the core: they insisted that veneration of nature was idolatry. The Jews backed away from nature and learned to look at the world outside themselves in terms of "other." They developed an objective point of view.

The Greek philosophers also contributed greatly to the objectification of nature. Their gods and goddesses were actors in an all-too-human manner: prone to jealousy, sexual exploits, killing, deceiving, and changing their minds. How could the Greeks make moral sense out of such a picture? Their way out of the dilemma was to form a mental universe of order by developing a particular form of intelligence called "reason." The scholar of religions, Huston Smith, has explained how all this came about, and he has pointed out that reason is based on division; that is, on making distinctions, on setting some things over against other things, and emphasizing control—which implies a distinction between the way things are and the way they ought to be re-ordered.[1]

If, as the philosophers did, you push things far enough away in your thought, they become "objects," rather than a part of your own feeling-world. You give up a sense of empathic connection with them. Then, they are held at arm's length, and may be conceived as separate. Huston Smith called this attitude of objectivity, "the decisive hallmark of the Western mind." It is symbolized in that first creation myth in Genesis, where God splits things in two. We then see things as distinguishable, as separate from one another.

A positive aspect of this objectification process is that, if objects exist independently, we may see them as interesting in their own right. We may seek to understand them and to manipulate or change them to suit our needs. However, as Huston Smith said, ". . . once the objective bent gets going, it knows no stop. Nothing is off limits. This objectifying tendency became generalized into a complete mental attitude. It got built into the idea of rationality itself . . . So when [the West] turns from the outer world to inner experience . . . the mind carries its objectivizing propensity with it. Thoughts come to be regarded as mental objects . . . feelings as 'data.'"[2] Wherever the Western mind ranges in thought, it casts whatever it encounters into the mold of objectifiable fact. So the Western mind is prone to confront reality as a totality of concrete, preferably picturable, objects, each separate from one another and from the mind that perceives it.

This objectifying tendency is encouraged by the structure of our language, our language being an obvious expression of our manner of thinking. From the day of Descartes on, Western philosophers explored various implications of the manner of perceiving implied by the subject-predicate and subject-verb-object form of speaking and writing. The most important implication is that the subject (self) may possess any number of qualities—"I am good-looking and intelligent, but prone to forgetfulness"— but it may seem to do so in isolation from other subjects. Subjects (selves), therefore, would seem to require nothing but themselves in order to exist. "I think, therefore, I am."

The structure of our language encourages us to believe that to be something real, actual, is to be an independent, ongoing individual with qualities of one's own. Any relatedness to other individuals is secondary. If your sense of your existence depends primarily on your awareness of yourself as a thinking individual, then you will conceive all others, human or nonhuman, in objective terms: they are "other than myself." What, then, is the nature of the connection between you and them? How are you related?

The goal of the objectifying tendency is clarity in order to control. But, as we Westerners are taught to see the world, it can only be controlled a bit at a time. That requires separation, division, and the reasoning that wants to command, master, and subject nature to one's will. A tiger can be tamed only by treating it as an "it," rather than a being much like ourselves.

We are also faced with this problem: we have so separated our sense of what *is* from our sense of what *ought* to be, that our ways of upholding those senses are in conflict: "what is" (our view of reality) is upheld by science, and "what ought to be" (our ethical sense) now flounders on a religious point of view that is not compatible with science and is no longer believed in by most educated people. What then? Is there a way of bringing the two back together? What place may we find for religion in an age of science?

[1] Huston Smith, *Essays on World Religion*. M. Darrol Bryant, editor. New York: Paragon House, 1992.
[2] Huston Smith, p. 193.

Chapter Two

Feeling Is First

It is essential to recognize the role of feeling in life. We start with ourselves and ask: what comes first, thinking or feeling?

In her book, *Mind: An Essay on Human Feeling*, the philosopher Susan Langer said that feeling is the mark of mentality. Understanding how it is that feeling comes before consciousness—and emotion before mind—is an essential undergirding of the philosophy upheld in this book.

The best-known proponent of that philosophy was Alfred North Whitehead, who did something unusual for a philosopher: he acknowledged the primary role of feeling in experience—and not just in human experience, but in any entity capable of having experience. He much expanded on our usual notions concerning the sorts of entities that are capable of experience. Following the American psychologist William James and foreshadowing the discoveries of contemporary cognitive scientists, Whitehead claimed that there is no such thing as a thought without a feeling prior to it, and that ". . . it is not true that we observe best when we are entirely devoid of emotion. Unless there is a direction of interest, we do not observe at all."[1] The task of understanding, then, is not to claim objectivity by denying the role of feeling, but, instead, to take feeling and emotion fully into account.

The most thorough treatment of the relationship between feeling and thought by a contemporary cognitive scientist may be found in Antonio Damasio's writing in *The Feeling of What Happens: Body and Emotion in the Making of Consciousness*. Damasio says that consciousness begins as a kind of feeling. He separates three stages of brain processing along a continuum: ". . . a state of emotion, which can be triggered and executed non-consciously; a state of feeling, which can be represented non-consciously (He does not explain how we could "represent" something non-consciously); and a state of feeling made conscious, i.e., known to the organism having both emotion and feeling."[2] The point I want to emphasize is that emotion is essentially a somatic (bodily) event and that the feeling of what happens is, primarily, the feeling of somatic events.

Instead of the usually accepted notion of emotion as "strong feeling" or "any specific feeling," which is reductionist, I prefer to define "emotion" in the physical sense that the term implies: (e-motion) the movement of energy in a body. It is this energy-movement that is *experienced* when we have feelings. Feelings are conscious sensations of emotion, so feelings require some degree of consciousness. I am highlighting the importance of understanding emotion as primary, it being the energy-movement that is sensed. Feeling is the sense of it. A feeling may be generalized, as in excitement or depression, or, to be more specific, as in sadness or anger.

Consciousness begins as a feeling. A *feeling process* is based on an *emotion process*. Both occur before a thought process can take place in a human being. This is as true for us as it is for ***every entity*** ever having a thought. In truth, there is no such thing as a thought without some emotion and feeling behind it.

Computers don't think. They process information. The popular idea that human thinking is nothing more than information-processing is reductionist. It overlooks the emotion and feeling that are the foundations of human thought. Much has been written in recent times about "emotional intelligence" as one of several forms of intelligence. What I am emphasizing is that *all* thinking has an emotional base. This realization is both philosophically and scientifically sound. It must not be lost sight of if we are to have an adequate view of the role of emotion, feeling, and consciousness in human life—and in the universe as a whole.

We can add this corollary: follow feeling where it leads, and you will discover that it never ends with yourself. Why feel anything if one is alone, cut off from the rest of creation? Why feel anything if everything outside of oneself is nothing but some object devoid of the feelings one has oneself or at least incapable of a feeling, a connection with oneself?

Consciousness begins as a feeling, and feeling is rooted in emotion. Emotion is our primary connection to the real world.

The primary ethical question is whether we are "moved" emotionally by the sufferings and joys of others.

---

[1] Alfred North Whitehead, *Religion in the Making*. New York: World, 1960 (originally 1929), p. 120f.
[2] Antonio Damasio, *The Feeling of What Happens: Body and Mind*

in the Making of Consciousness. San Diego: Harcourt, 1999, p. 37.

Chapter Three

What Is a Self?

An old Buddhist view of the nature of the self is supported by modern cognitive science. Even so, both versions are inadequate.

What is a self? How does it arise? How is it maintained? These questions are being vigorously investigated and debated by biochemists, neuroscientists, psychologists, and philosophers. Contemporary cognitive science would seem to confirm the judgment of existentialist philosophy that there is no such thing as a self, prior to experience. How, then, are we to think about selves as they relate to other selves and to other entities that we may not regard as selves?

In order to answer this question, the philosopher Alfred North Whitehead adopted an old Buddhist view of the self: the self (or soul) is *not* a single actual entity, remaining as one essence throughout time (as Hindu, Greek and Christian philosophies taught), but is, rather, a "society" of momentary occasions of experience. Only one such occasion occurs at any one time. Each momentary occasion of the self is related to antecedent and subsequent occasions that serve to create the ongoing sense of self.

It is important to understand that this relationship of self-occasions is something more than mere causal influence. Each moment of experience actually includes or incorporates its precedents into itself, and then remains "present" in some manner within all succeeding experiences. That is both the Buddhist and the modern process philosophy teaching.

Just as the Buddhists' denial of an enduring underlying substance, or "atman," allowed them to affirm such a "social" doctrine of the person, in much the same manner does quantum physics see the actual entities of the physical world. The world of quantum physics is a world of discrete events, each of which occurs in relation to all other events. Whitehead saw the nature of the human self in the same way: each self-event is related to all other self-events.

This way of looking at the concept of the self has us seeing two related processes going on in the self—as in the Universe at large—from the beginning: differentiation and subjectivity. Differentiation and subjectivity go together. As soon as things get differentiated—formed as separated entities (electrons, atoms, cells, whatever)—they become capable of some degree of subjectivity—not in the common sense of "lacking in reality or substance," but rather the opposite: something "of which a quality, attribute or relation may be affirmed or in which it may inhere."[1] What it comes to is this: *the reality of subjectivity is in the relationships the subject has with other subjects.* So what we call "objects" should be thought of as (in some cases, aggregations of) subjects, capable of influencing and being influenced by other subjects and, thus, having relations with them. There is only one subject that can exist without relationship to others: the entire Universe. And subjects don't exist as static things but, instead, as a series of occasions constituting a process.

Today's cognitive scientists see this happening in neurological processes. For example, Daniel Dennett describes the self as a "center of narrative gravity," which is itself "gappy," that is, functioning in discrete processes like those of quantum physics. While consciousness may appear to be continuous, our selves are what the ancient Buddhists said they are: not things that last, but experiences that are tied together by the relationships between those experiences.

If your self is a process of occasions of experience, rather than a single ongoing entity, then, therefore, the old dualistic view, which still prevails in common thinking, is wrong. Descartes said, "I think; therefore, I am," insisting that body and mind (or self, or soul) are different things. His "I" was not made of flesh and bone, but was something mysterious, some single ongoing entity that, though not physical, somehow interacted intimately with his flesh and bone. The prevailing view today is that science overwhelmingly refutes Descartes. "I am; therefore, I think," is the modern view.

The modern view presents us with some new issues. For example, if self-consciousness may be explained in terms of the workings of what Daniel Dennett calls a "virtual machine, a sort of evolved (and evolving) computer program that shapes the activities of the brain," then ". . . in principle, a suitable 'programmed' robot, with a silicon-based computer brain, would be conscious, would have a self.[2] And if the "you" in yourself is, in reality, nothing but the functioning of a very complicated, evolved machine made of organic molecules instead of metal and silicone, then there is no reason to think that a conscious machine might not someday be made. Books like *The Age of Spiritual Machines: When Computers Exceed Human Intelligence*, by Ray Kurzweil (1998), explain why and how all this will inevitably occur. He wrote that, by 2019, a $1,000 computer would match the processing power of the human brain and that people would have relationships with electronic "personalities" as companions, teachers, caregivers, even lovers! He also predicted that a computer-driven machine will pass the Turing Test, i.e., be able to convince a human conversationalist of its conscious character. He believed that, by 2029, *most* of our communication will be with machines that will be capable even of a "feeling "of transcending one's everyday physical and mortal bounds to "sense a deeper reality"- that is, spiritual experience! It is now 2019, and it seems his predictions were over-stated.

I recommend Bill McKibben's book, *Falter*, for a discussion of the dangers of artificial intelligence.

Such mind-boggling predictions as Kurzwell's are based on a well-established trend: the prowess of computers has usually come about earlier, rather than later, than predicted. But spiritual experience? We may reasonably doubt it. The main reason for doubting it is a major theme of this book: the crucial role of feeling in self-consciousness, indeed, in all kinds of consciousness. Feeling is first, and computers don't feel. Yes, people have been fooled into believing that they have been communicating with a machine that must have been feeling something; whereas, in fact, it was only a machine and it didn't feel a thing.

There can be no self without feeling, but feeling doesn't require a brain. From a biologist's point of view, even a single-celled bacterium qualifies as a self: a unit of life that is organized to nourish itself and protect itself from attack by non-selves. Selves, first of all, are feeling entities. Selves are capable of sensing non-selves and reacting to them. Brains are not required—feeling is. And feeling permeates the natural world. Rather than insisting on its dependence upon a complicated brain, this way of thinking enables us to see selfhood exhibited over the widest possible range of subjectivity—all the way from cells to the incredible complexity of the human (or dolphin) brain.

A bacterium is a simple self. Multi-celled plants and animals are, obviously, more complicated. Our bodies are colonies of trillions of cells that share the identity of a single self. Colonies of social insects such as ants have several levels of selfhood.

Those who insist that a brain is required for self-identity should explain how it is that, to a DNA scientist, a bit of your skin is recognizably you. Your immune system recognizes *non-yous*, or you're in trouble. Evolving nervous systems gave rise to the human brain—and to your own self-awareness, which is something plants and—all but the big-brained animals don't seem to have. They have selves and a rudimentary consciousness but lack self-awareness or "high-level" consciousness. *Selfhood and consciousness are matters of degree.*

Scientists see the human self as arising solely out of biological evolution. Even so, some scientists cannot resist the temptation to wax poetic: "The human self is not a dualism of mind and matter, but rather an efflorescence of self from matter . . . a shimmering exuberance of the stuff of the universe gathered in the human brain into biochemical webs of astonishing complexity."[3] I'd call that a "radiant materialism." But is materialism an adequate view regarding self, feeling, and consciousness?

What's more, if a self isn't a real thing, but only a sort of construction of experiences, what happens to moral responsibility? One of the most important roles of a self—in our traditional belief—is the place where the buck stops. As Daniel Dennett puts it, ". . . if there is no Oval Office in the brain housing a Highest Authority to whom all decisions can be appealed, we seem to be threatened with a Kafkaesque bureaucracy of homunculi, who always reply when challenged, 'Don't blame me, I just work here.' The task of constructing a self that can take responsibility is a major social and educational project . . . The only hope, and not at all a forlorn one, is to come to understand, naturalistically, the ways in which brains group self-representations, thereby equipping the bodies they control with responsible selves when all goes well" (Dennett, p. 429f).

How could such an understanding ever meet the issue of responsibility? Missing in such a view is the sense of *feeling connection* with other selves that I am emphasizing.

[1]Merriam Webster's *Collegiate Dictionary*, 10th edition.
[2]Daniel C. Dennett, *Consciousness Explained*, Boston, Little, Brown & Co., 1991, p. 431.
[3]Chet Raymo, *Boston Globe*, "Science Musings," 11/27/2001.

Chapter Four

Is Mind More Than What Brains Do?

The materialist's case for "mind equals brain-function" is unconvincing in view of recent research. The nature of mind is much more extensive than is usually thought. If emotion is our primary connection to the real world, mind runs it a close second.

"Consciousness contemplates no more profound or perplexing question than this: what is its role in the establishment of reality?" ~*Robert G. Jahn and Brenda J. Dunne,* **Margins of Reality**

In his book, *The Healing Wisdom of Africa*, Malidoma Patrice Somé upholds a fascinating reversal of the usual Western view of the role of consciousness in the world: for his native Dagara people, ". . . there is an understood hierarchy of consciousness. The elements of nature, especially the trees and plants, are the most intelligent beings because they do not need words to communicate. They live closer to the meanings behind language. The next most intelligent species are the animals because they use only a minimum of uttered communication, so their language is closer to the Source, the world of intrinsic meaning. The last in the hierarchy is the human species, who must rely on words to communicate—and words are but a remote reflection of meaning, like the shadows on the wall of Plato's cave."[1]

Civilized folk are far removed from such a conception of consciousness. Rather than regarding nature as profoundly intelligent in itself, we have come to look on nature as composed of raw material that waits to be exploited for our benefit. Western humankind has viewed the notion of progress in terms of the extent of its separation from the world of nature even though that separation is an illusion.

One important reason for the illusion of oneself as separate from the world, rather than tied into a web of relationships, has been the dualistic belief that the self is different in kind from the world known through sensory perception. It became the custom in Western thought to see the human self, and it alone, as characterized by consciousness. Gradually the realization has taken hold that at least some nonhuman animals are more than machines. They are soulful. The Rev. Mr. Gary Kowalski speaks to this point in his beautiful book, *The Souls of Animals*.

Animals have thoughts as well as feelings. Naturalist, Bernd Heinrich, has studied ravens for many years and has concluded from observation of their behaviors that they are capable of thinking ahead and acting on those thoughts, of acting appropriately in novel situations. In his book, *Mind of the Raven*, he points out that intelligence involves testing responses in the mind before acting them out in a dangerous world. Ravens can show such awareness and understanding.

Even so, people persist in the belief that most of the world consists of bits of matter that are completely devoid of experience. Matter, they insist, is purely objective. They reason that, unlike thinking and feeling animals, the world of matter has no inner, subjective, private side. One of the problems created by that idea was noticed from the outset: the mind-body problem. How could two essentially different types of substances (mind and body) be conceived as interacting? Where's the connection? The most widely adopted approach in modern times to the problem of *mind* has been to assume that the problem was caused by Descartes' view of the mind as a distinct non-physical substance or actuality; whereas, the mind is now generally regarded by cognitive scientists as a property or function of the brain—nothing more than what the brain does.

This is not a new view. Hippocrates (460-370 B.C.E.) wrote: "Men ought to know that from nothing else but the brain come joys, delights, laughter and sports, and sorrows, griefs, despondency and lamentations"—quoted by Francis Crick, who begins his own writing: "The Astonishing Hypothesis is that 'You,' your joys and your sorrows, your memories and your ambitions, your sense of personal identity and free will, are, in fact, no more than the behavior of a vast assembly of nerve cells and their associated molecules"(Francis Crick, *The Astonishing Hypothesis.* NY: Simon and Schuster, 1994, p. 3).

According to the prevailing scientific view, consciousness depends entirely upon a brain; it is no more than brain function. These activities are not thought to be products of a centralized system, but rather, of a sort of confederation. This is to say, there is "no one in charge" inside our brains, no physical or even psychological center of activity. There is only a web-like connection of processes. As Daniel Dennett put it, "We must admit that genuine understanding is somehow achieved by a process composed of interactions between a host of subsystems none of which understand a thing by themselves."[2]

How can this be? How could some information-processing event in your brain *be* the delicious scent of a warm summer breeze that you feel on your skin? If there's nobody inside watching or otherwise experiencing brain events, how may a purely physical organ perform functions, such as, perceive a red rose, appreciate wine, reject racism, perform mathematical calculations, love someone, or act out of moral responsibility? The answer of contemporary cognitive science is: the brain does it all. And without feeling a thing.

Having read several books on this subject, I am (with this second edition) now not up-to-date regarding what neuroscientists are thinking. In 2000, Gerald Edelman and Giulio Tononi told us that our brains work by means of "a cluster of neuronal groups that are strongly interacting among themselves and that have distinct functional borders with the rest of the brain at the time scale of a fraction of a second." They call this "cluster" a "dynamic core" and emphasize both its integration and its constantly changing composition. "A dynamic core is therefore a process, not a thing or place, and it is defined in terms of neural interactions, rather than in terms of specific neural location, connectivity, or activity." It is spatially distributed, as well as constantly changing, and, therefore, cannot be localized (*A Universe of Consciousness:*

How Matter Becomes Imagination. NY. Basic Books, 2000, p. 144). Edelman and Tononi believe this concept of dynamic core helps to answer the "qualia" question: *how can the physical brain provide us with subjective experiences of color, warmth, pain, a loud sound, and so on?* They say that each qualia "corresponds to" a different state of the dynamic core (p. 157). It is the use of terms like "corresponds to" that I find puzzling. Does this mean that subjective experiences amount to such energetic states, no more, nor less? This seems to be their view. They offer no other. And we are left with the mystery as we read further. For example, "the simplest way to address the problem of qualia is to assume that for every quale, all that is needed is a group of neurons, or even a single neuron, that, when firing, explicitly represents a particular aspect of consciousness or quale" (p. 163).

What does it mean for a physical process to "represent" a person seeing red or feeling warm or hearing a loud sound? Much has been written in an attempt to answer this question. Edelman and Tononi address the issue: why should the firing of certain neurons generate, let's say, "redness" and not some other quale, like a painful feeling? "And why should it generate a quale at all when firings of neurons in the retina or in the lateral geniculate nucleus appear to generate nothing in the way of subjective feelings? ... If we take the *one neuronal group, one quale* approach, these questions remain unanswered. Back then, to the "dynamic core" hypotheses whereby "perceiving the redness of red absolutely requires a discrimination among integrated states of the entire "dynamic core . . . (p. 167). In other words, even simple subjective states turn out to be very complicated. Edelman and Tononi push this view to a logical conclusion: "every different conscious state deserves to be called a quale . . . the meaning of the conscious perception is given by the discrimination among billions of other possible states of the core, each of which would lead to different consequences. This is exactly what we mean when we say that consciousness is informative" (p. 168).

It seems that we have a lot of discrimination going on, all the time, in our brain-minds. This implies a lot of decision-making: something decides what to discard, if the brain is to have any focus. One out of billions of potential "qualia"—for example, what you see when you see a colored object—must prevail, at each moment. What is (are) the deciding factor(s)? How are we to explain our power of self-determination or ability to exert any influence upon our own thinking?

Recent writings by neuroscientists point toward such explanation, but we are not out of the woods yet. For one thing, even with the thoroughgoing materialism of the "mind equals brain" position, a troublesome sort of dualism still haunts us regarding two sorts of actualities: those with and those without experience. How are we to explain a brain, or any physical entity, as having experience? How may it be shown that the firing of neurons is all there is to our thoughts and feelings?

Antonio Damasio revisited this question in an Appendix, "Notes on Mind and Brain," in his book, *The Feeling of What Happens* where he tries to distinguish between an image and a neural pattern: "When I use the term *image*, I always mean *mental* image. A synonym for image is *mental pattern*. I do not use the word image to refer to the pattern of neural activities . . ." For that—he reserves the term, "neural pattern or map." Then we find this important admission: "There is a mystery, however, regarding *how* images emerge from neural patterns. How a neural pattern *becomes* an image is a problem that neurobiology has not yet resolved."[3] I suggest that the reader revisit that last sentence.

That, it seems to me, is the crux of the matter. How can the firing of neurons in a brain become an image—something that we can see? Perhaps more recent writings help to clarify this issue; otherwise, we are left with a mystery.

The mind is *at least* "what the brain does." As Stephen Pinker puts it: "The mind is a system of organs of computation, designed by natural selection to solve the kinds of problems our ancestors faced in their foraging way of life, in particular, understanding and outmaneuvering objects, animals, plants, and other people . . . the brain processes information, and thinking is a kind of computation. The mind is organized into modules or mental organs, each with a specialized design that makes it an expert in one arena of interaction with the world" (Stephen Pinker, *How the Mind Works*. NY: W.W. Norton & Co. 1997, p. 21). Pinker believes the "computational" theory resolves the mind-body problem: how to connect the ethereal world of meaning and intention with a physical hunk of matter, like the brain. The computational theory says that ". . . beliefs and desires are *information*, incarnated as configurations of symbols. The symbols are the physical states of bits of matter . . . They symbolize things in the world because they are triggered by those things via our sense organs, and because of what they do once they are triggered . . . The computational theory of mind thus allows us to keep beliefs and desires in our explanations of behavior while planting them squarely in the physical universe. It allows meaning to cause and be caused."[8]

Does it, really? Scientists disagree concerning the brain as a sort of supercomputer. Recent developments in cognitive science suggest that human intelligence is utterly different from machine or artificial intelligence. Computers process information in a completely mechanistic manner. As we have seen, the human nervous system's activity is always driven by emotions, bodily sensations, and processes. A lot goes on in your head when you have a thought. A good deal of it is information having a complexity that is far beyond the capabilities of present-day computers.

This is an urgent concern as increasingly all forms of human culture are being subordinated to technological innovation. We need, for example, to be careful about using computers in our schools. Humans think with ideas, not information. All meaningful knowledge is contextual, and computers know nothing about context. It is also important to understand that the language used by computers is full of metaphors derived from the military: "command," "escape," "target," and so forth—language that reinforces unhealthy stereotypes. A related issue is the connection between computers and the violent nature of most computer-based games, which capture the attention of America's children. Computer language also includes sexist terms.

Perhaps you've seen enough of the prevailing materialist view of mental activity. Opposing views are held by a significant number of people with good scientific training who are not convinced of the prevailing belief, that the unitary, private nature of consciousness is its foremost property and that each conscious event has a single point of view, which cannot be shared. Cognitive scientists insist that the mind arises from the body and its development—and that attempts to imbue the world at large with conscious properties must be ruled out. Must we do so?

What, for example, are we to make of the physicist, Fritjof Capra's view of cognition as "the process of life?" He says that ". . . the organizing activity of living systems, at all levels of life, is mental activity." He sees the interactions of living organisms with their environment as "cognitive, or mental interactions." He believes that "Mind—or more accurately, mental process—is immanent in matter at all levels of life." How could that be the case?

Capra discusses the contributions of Gregory Bateson and Humberto Maturana to support the belief that the various mental processes are a necessary and inevitable consequence of a complex development that begins long before organisms develop brains and higher nervous systems. He insists that ". . . the brain is not necessary for mind to exist. A bacterium, or a plant, has no brain but has a mind. The simplest organisms are capable of perception and, thus, of cognition. They do not see, but they nevertheless perceive changes in their environment—differences between light and shadow, hot and cold, higher and lower concentrations of some chemical, and the like. The new concept of cognition, the process of knowing, is, thus, much broader than that of thinking. It involves perception, emotion, and action—

the entire process of life."[4]

The mind is surely a process, and the brain is a specific structure by means of which this process operates. May we generalize from our own "inside" events of consciousness and feeling to the presumed "inside" of events outside of ourselves that we don't know from inside but which seem similar—since the entities having those experiences act as though they have "insides" much like our own?

The philosopher Thomas Nagel wrote a famous essay, "What Is It Like to Be a Bat?" And the philosopher Leibniz tried to explain what it is like to be an atom. We may be inclined to pursue such an inquiry, if we can conceive of even atoms as, somehow, "centers of feeling." That's a big leap. The first step would be to recognize that, like us, atoms are "temporarily ordered societies of distinct events," as A.N. Whitehead put it. That's what quantum physics teaches. However, most quantum physicists do not draw the conclusion that all actualities are capable of some degree of perception. It is usually assumed that perception is essentially sense perception, and, therefore, can only be attributed to organisms with sense organs. But what if sense perception is derivative from a more primitive form of experience, where something is felt without the subject—knowing it in the sense that we know it? What would that be? It would seem to be some sort of sympathetic energetic resonance, where two or more subjects are affected by the others' excited state.

It has been assumed that all experience involves consciousness. Is that so? Certainly, consciousness presupposes experience, but is the reverse also the case?

Can it not be, as Whitehead suggested, that, in fact, an occasion of experience may have several phases, with consciousness arising at a relatively advanced stage, and self-consciousness developing late in evolution? Perhaps the problem is that we are too accustomed to thinking of consciousness as the sort of "stuff" out of which thoughts are made.

Consciousness is a function of experience, the function of knowing. Lack of consciousness does not entail lack of experience—or lack of feeling—only an inability to comprehend or analyze our experience. What else is there in the Universe but "occasions of experience?" It would be hard indeed to conceive of any such thing.

A recent understanding of brain function has it that the brain reads information by transforming images that it gets from the world into wave interference patterns and then by transforming them again into virtual images, just as a laser hologram does. If so, when we see, we are creating and projecting an image of the object into the same space as the object so that the object and our perception coincide. In this act of observation, we are actually transforming the timeless, space-less world of wave interference patterns into the discrete world of space and time. According to that view, our memories are stored, not in localized areas of the brain, but throughout the brain and body in the form of wave patterns—which is a remarkably efficient arrangement, since the weak electromagnetic waves of the energy-field we inhabit can hold unimaginable amounts of information. At its core, then, consciousness is not a matter of chemistry, but of "coherent light." Consciousness, including memory, resides, first of all, in the all-pervasive energy-field. Our brains are "retrieval mechanisms." Lynne McTaggart's book, *The Field*, summarizes research that upholds this view.

I think that this view has much to commend it. It is upheld by research into "mind-extension" that has taken place in several university settings over many years by reputable scientists. Scientists at the Princeton (University) Engineering Anomalies Research Laboratory (and elsewhere) are making a strong case for such parapsychological phenomena as "precognitive remote perception." For example, someone sitting in a room in Princeton generates and records impressions of a scene viewed somewhere else by someone else—*before* the scene is visited, and even before it is selected!

Robert G. Jahn and Brenda J. Dunne explain such "anomalous" phenomena in scientific terms. Their definition of consciousness is certainly more expansive than that of the cognitive scientists—but it resonates with the statements of some biologists and theoretical physicists: "The distinction between living and nonliving systems, or between systems capable of 'consciousness' or not, is becoming progressively more diffuse when approached from either the biological or physical perspective. Such biological entities as viruses, coacervates, and the life-forming DNA and RNA structures lie in a twilight zone between elaborate chemical complexes and vitally competent organisms . . . The most fundamental premise of this model—that reality is established only in the interaction of a consciousness with its environment—need not be formally constrained to consciousness associated with a living system . . . any functioning entity capable of generating, receiving, or utilizing information qualifies as a consciousness."⁵

We will pursue this question further (in Part IV, Chapter Four). The question is, what is the relationship between emotion, feeling and thought, and are feelings (awareness of emotion) and thoughts necessarily confined to individual brain processes? Or is there some manner by which energy movement beyond the confines of brains can carry feeling and thought from living entities to other living entities? Is there is a reality to such "pan-psychism" that is not supernaturally mystical, but naturally energetic?

¹Malidoma Patrice Somé, *The Healing Wisdom of Africa*. NY: Tarcher/Putnam Inc., 1998, p, 50.
²Dan Dennett, *Consciousness Explained*. Boston: Little Brown & Co., 1991, p.438f.
³Antonio Damasio, *The Feeling of What Happens*. San Diego: Harcourt, Inc., 1999, p. 317.
⁴Fritjof Capra, *The Web of Life*. NY: Anchor Books, 1966. P. 174f.
⁵Robert G. Jahn and Brenda J. Dunne, Margins of Reality, San Diego: Harcourt Brace & Co., 1987, p. 257f.

Chapter Five

Religion and Sexuality

Our connection to the natural world is broken whenever our sexual energy is suppressed, sublimated, or distorted.

I have made a case for human connection to the real world by means of emotion and thought. An important form of our emotional connection is felt as sexual energy. The way we think about the expression of this energy determines much of our attitude toward ourselves and the rest of nature.

One of the characteristics of a natural religion is a healthy attitude toward sexuality. In the animistic religions, there is no conflict between religion and sexuality. The trouble began when the patriarchal, warrior, male gods—of the Aryans in India, the Norsemen in Northern Europe, and the Hebrews in the Middle East—invented and enforced a separation between heaven and earth, the life of the body and that of the spirit, and put us at war with ourselves and with nature. They associated sexuality with women, and the goddess, who represented nature. When they suppressed the goddess and oppressed women, they distorted the natural function of sexuality and turned it into something perverse and pornographic.

It is no mere coincidence that an important part of the

definition of a saint includes the sublimation, if not complete suppression, of sexual desire. The Christian idea of original sin has as its core the repression of pleasurable sexual excitation (represented by the serpent) and its replacement with obedience to God's representatives, the priests or ministers, who alone are qualified to interpret scripture. In such a context, it can be more important to control the reproductive lives of women than it is to deal with overpopulation or economic injustice. To be human is to be sexual. It we are to bring religion and sexuality back together in a healthy manner, we will have to find a way to make peace with ourselves and with nature.

As we saw near the beginning of this book, in Christianity, as in Essene Judaism, the idea of original sin was developed out of an insistence on the division of the human person into two warring components: soul versus body, spirit versus nature, where the sinful nature of the body was characterized primarily in anti-sexual and anti-feminine terms. This wounding of human nature was founded on the repression of pleasurable sexual excitation as sex became more and more associated with degrading earthly matters that impede the striving for a heavenly realm. This sad condition was increased when, over centuries, sex-negative attitudes and childrearing rendered full, natural sexual pleasure unattainable, and substitute measures for obtaining gratification developed as a result. In the name of various religions and political movements, people were encouraged or even forced to channel their sexual energies into activities for the furtherance of those movements.

Despite his atheism, Sigmund Freud agreed with the orthodox Christians in viewing the human as alien to the rest of nature. Like them, he was unable to accept humans as well-rooted in the physical world. Freud summed up his civilized attitude toward nature when he wrote: "Against the dreaded external world one can only defend oneself by some kind of turning away from it if one intends to solve the task by oneself. There is, indeed, another and better path: that of becoming a member of the human community, and, with the help of a technique guided by science, going over to the attack against nature and subjecting her to the human will"— from his *Civilization and Its Discontents*. Like the religious folk, Dr. Freud seems to have had no idea of the disastrous consequences of such an attitude.

Those consequences are now clear. Rather than the splendor of creation, we humans have become a noxious form of life, a sort of cancer, spreading over the earth, consuming as we go, to the point where we are causing irredeemable harm to the entire earth community. If the other creatures could have their say, they would surely vote to have us quarantined as too deadly a presence to be let loose.

We have seen the development of the human anti-nature attitude in religion. Clarification of its emergence in Western culture was provided as early as 1942 by Wilhelm Reich in *The Mass Psychology of Fascism*. In this important work, much read in its day, Reich explained how ideas and feelings about God and sexuality are closely related in unarmored individuals—those whose bodies are not blocked energetically. Much of Reich's work was devoted to understanding how armoring develops and how it can be responsibly removed through therapy.

In "primitive" (animistic) religions, there is no conflict

between religious and sexual feelings. But when, along with the patriarchal suppression of an earlier goddess-oriented culture, society became armored, that unity of feeling became dissociated, and religion became antithetical to sexuality. The sexual feelings of the individual were repressed and became opposed to religious feelings. Once that separation was solidified in the form of character armor, religious excitation assumed a new function: that of being a substitute for the lost sexual pleasure, no longer affirmed by society. So the energy source of religious fervor is repressed sexual excitation.

We see the disastrous consequences of this armoring in the perverse "acting out" of repressed and distorted sexual feeling both by priests who abuse unsuspecting young people and by terrorists who have submerged themselves in religiously charged fundamentalist fantasies.

According to Reich, the structure of the mystical individual can be described as follows: "Biologically, he is subject to states of sexual tension like any other living being. But, through the assimilation of the sex-negating religious ideas in general and the fear of punishment in particular, he has lost all capacity for natural sexual excitation and gratification. As a result, he suffers from a chronic state of excessive somatic excitation that he is constantly forced to master. Happiness in this world is not only unattainable for him, but it does not even seem desirable to him. Since he expects happiness in the hereafter, he develops a feeling of being incapable of happiness in this world. But, being a biological organism and thus unable to renounce happiness, relaxation and satisfaction, there is only one thing left for him to do: to seek the illusory happiness provided by the religious fore-pleasure excitations . . ."[1]

An extreme case of this armored condition is that of the Islamic fundamentalist who turns to terrorism. In order to understand the roots of such terrorism, it is not enough to think politically or sociologically. We must see how such terrorism amounts to a perverted expression of the terrorist's need to avoid, at all costs, the terror of his own energy streamings.

The degree of sexual repression and frustration produced by the Islamic fundamentalists is more severe than with the orthodox sects of Judeo-Christianity because in fundamentalist Islamic countries there is no separation between religion and state, and punishment for transgressions of extremist Islamic law is severe. In such fundamentalist settings, men and women cannot show affection in public; women are veiled and subject to all sorts of restrictions and even clitorectomies (but men are permitted to initiate a kiss and hold hands). Sexual feelings can be partially discharged through emotionally voiced prayers and heated discussions of Islamic ideology. The denial of the sexual nature of such excitations results in insincerity.

One problem with such religious insincerity is that it often seems so sincere. The way to get at the truth of that issue is to inquire into the person's view of sexuality and nature, and also of women and feminine functions. There is something inherently evasive in the patriarchal point of view as Reich pointed out many years ago.

Reich focused on sexual repression within the authoritarian family, as the breeding-ground for fascism. "The patriarchal authoritarian sexual order . . . becomes the primary basis of authoritarian ideology by depriving the women, children, and adolescents of their sexual freedom, making a commodity of sex and placing sexual interests in the service of economic subjugation . . . Surrounded by and imbued with human sexual structures that have become distorted and lascivious, patriarchal man is shackled . . . in an ideology in which sexual and dirty, sexual and vulgar or demonic, become inseparable associations" (*The Mass Psychology of Fascism*, p. 88).

[1] Wilhelm Reich, *The Mass Psychology of Fascism*. New York: Noonday, 1970 edition, p. 125.

Chapter Six

The Promise of Human Nature

Does the wounded-ness of human nature in our culture leave room for optimism? Altruism is a test case.

"Anna and I learned a lot about the human heart this year. We learned it can hold more than we thought possible. We learned it can grow." ~*Frances Moore Lappé and Anna Lappé in* **Hope's Edge**[1]

Many years after Wilhelm Reich clarified the perniciousness of patriarchy, and several years after the archaeologist Marija Gimbutas provided extensive documentation of patriarchy's domination over an earlier more benign human culture, it has become commonplace to see the dominance of patriarchy in many facets of human life. Many authors, of both male and female identities, have written to the effect that, for the most part, men have governed without respect for the well-being of women or of the earth.

What is the result of all the progress made possible over the centuries by the patriarchal establishments? Despite its many achievements, a patriarchal culture has alienated us from nature and produced a level of destructiveness far beyond anything previously known in human history.

How, then, may we speak of the promise of human nature? How may we affirm "the inherent worth and dignity" of human beings, as religious liberals do? If we human beings are worthy by nature and have inherent dignity, how did we get ourselves into such a slew of trouble? Why are people so thoughtless, so inconsiderate, and so destructive? As we have seen, a religious doctrine of sinfulness and a psychological theory of a death wish are both attempts to explain something we see all around us: human greed, violence, and trashing of the environment. How else to explain such things?

A lot rests on our deliberations. If we're as bad or flawed as some people say, there's no good reason to hope for our future. If not, what sort of worth or dignity is inherent in us, and what's the evidence of it? It's the old nature versus nurture controversy. Some will say that people do bad things because we're all born bad, or, at least, flawed in some essential way. Orthodox Christian theology and Freudian psychology are examples of that "fallen" or "flawed nature" view. People holding such a view are hard-pressed to explain why so many people don't do bad things, and, instead, do a great many good things.

Those holding to the nurture (or lack of it) explanation will say that people who do bad things have been warped in some way through ill-treatment and/or neglect as infants, children and adolescents. Liberals in religion and psychology hold such a view. Though not a liberal, Wilhelm Reich provided a persuasive defense for that position. He explained how a mistreated child will form a secondary, defensive, layer of "character armor," which manifests as a distortion of the decent core of the individual. It is that distortion that houses the fear, sadness and rage that we view as troublesome.

By contrast, when we are able to observe infants and young children who are well treated, we find that they are living contradictions of the "bad by nature" view. They are full of life! They are interested in everything around them. They are clearly and honestly expressive of their feelings. They are full of fun, and even soulful, in their pensive moments. Perhaps you can recall an occasion when a very young person spoke or sang or played a musical instrument in a way that impressed you as incorporating a mature sort of wisdom.

When you hear or read of the upbringing—really, the *downtrodding*—of the murderers, rapists, and torturers, what do you find? In each and every case, the more you learn, the more it's, "No wonder!" No wonder, considering how that person was treated, that the need for revenge was so great. The wonder is, how have others who were treated as poorly kept from behaving that way? Again, the more you learn, the clearer it gets. The one who, somehow, remained fairly decent, though treated very badly, had some better fortune, someone who cared or helped enough to keep them from going off the deep end.

Philosophers and psychologists have debated this issue for a long time. Often they have focused on the question of altruism as the "test case." *Unto Others: The Evolution and Psychology of Unselfish Behavior*, by Elliot Sober, a philosopher, and David Sloan Wilson, a biologist, is a serious treatment of this subject. Recognizing that, "As the most facultative species on earth, human beings appear willing and able to span the full spectrum from mercilessly exploiting their social partners to sacrificing their lives for others,"[2] they make the case for altruism as one of the important characteristics of humanity. As illustration, they point to Stephen Crane's short story, "The Open Boat," which was based on a real-life event.

Crane was a passenger on a ship that sank in a storm off the coast of Florida. He found himself in a dingy with the captain and two other members of the crew. With the boat riding only a few inches above the water and frequently swamped by heavy seas, Crane took turns rowing toward shore. He endured more pain and fatigue than he thought possible; when he could no longer row, trading places required the most careful movements to avoid upsetting the craft. Here is a part of his account of how he felt toward the other members of the group who had been total strangers only a few hours before: "It is difficult to describe the subtle brotherhood of men that was here established on the seas . . . It was more than a mere recognition of what was best for the common safety. There was surely in it a quality that was personal and heartfelt. After this devotion to the commander of the boat, there was this comradeship, that the correspondent, for instance, who had been taught to be cynical of men, knew even at the time was the best experience of his life."

People who have had such an experience will often characterize it as the best of their lives. This goes far beyond any egoistic or hedonistic concern. It can only be due to a strongly felt sense of connection, a comradeship that the person may never have experienced before and finds hard to put into words.

Consider the soldier in a foxhole who throws himself

on a live grenade to save the lives of his comrades, or a young woman who loses her life while rescuing a child who had run in front of an oncoming car. Suppose neither of these people believes in a life after death. Holders of the hedonist philosophy (who insist that a desire to promote pleasure and avoid pain is the ultimate reason for altruism) will suggest that a self-sacrificing person still benefits because his/her decision is less painful than a decision to let someone die. But isn't that stretching the point too far? For one thing, in such cases, there is usually no time for a thoughtful decision. The tendency is to act "impulsively." What is the basis of such an impulse? It can only be an ingrained sense of connection, a feeling of the "other" and the self as in some essential manner being the same—that the same life lives through all of us, and binds us together. When such "heroes" survive the experience, the last thing they want is to be called heroes. They will usually say that they had no time to think; they just did what came naturally to them. They will even ask: "Wouldn't anyone do the same?" That question, embarrassing though it may be to the hearer, assumes the inherent worth and dignity of the human being.

Sober and Wilson explore altruism from the view of psychology, evolution and biology. Regarding the last of these, Boyce Rensberger's *Life Itself: Exploring the Realm of the Living Cell* (1997) offers the concept that the body of an organism should be viewed as a "republic of cells" in which "a huge colony of extraordinarily selfless citizens" (the cells) have each forsaken an independent existence to create the self-sustaining individual. This informs our understanding of what happens when individual cells "revolt" and undergo changes to "pursue renegade causes," such as cancer. Of course, this is not to say that our (healthy) cells are altruistic in the fully philosophical sense. But it is a way of seeing how self-sacrifice for the good of others—or for the good of the larger whole of which we may feel ourselves to be a significant part—is rooted in our biology.

Altruism is also rooted in our evolution, as some recent research suggests. A psychiatrist at Emory University has written of the discovery that acts of cooperation, of choosing trust over cynicism, generosity over selfishness, actually makes the brain light up with a sort of "quiet joy."[3] Mental circuitry associated with reward-seeking behavior is stimulated when people choose mutualism over "me-ism." This is not true for everyone. 20- 39% of people who play such laboratory games ("The Prisoner's Dilemma") are prone to cruel punishment and competition, rather than kindness and cooperation. What Reich called their destructive "secondary layer" is well solidified. But most of us cooperate, and it feels good to do it. I did *not* write: "most of us cooperate *because* it feels good to do it." That hedonistic interpretation would be misplaced. The fact that it feels good may incline us to repeat such behavior, but our reasons for behaving altruistically are other-directed. We don't have ourselves in mind; we have other people in mind.

Why are humans as nice as we usually are? Why do we cooperate with people whom we barely know? Why do we play fair most of the time? Scientists have no trouble explaining the evolution of competitive behavior. But the depth and breadth of human goodness, the willingness to forego immediate personal gain for the long-term common goal, far exceeds what would be predicted from a hedonistic or pessimistic view of human nature.

Altruism is not something foreign to us as human beings—as long as we remain rooted in nature. Like the other animals, people do things for any of a number of reasons. The most compelling reason is that altruism is an expression of the feeling of connection with others, a feeling strong enough to lead someone to self-sacrifice under some conditions.

From such considerations as these, we may reasonably conclude that the promise of human nature depends, first of all, on our willingness and ability to accept ourselves as parts of the natural world. Without that rootedness, we lose all sense of those outside our bodies as other worthy ways in which life expresses itself. If we cannot feel others as like ourselves in worth and dignity, they become mere objects to us, and we lose our own dignity by becoming selfish, uncaring, and even destructive.

That is the view, not only of indigenous people like the native Americans, but also of social justice activists in many of the churches and a growing number of Americans who are getting fed up with the great disparity between rich and poor in one of the wealthiest nations on earth. It can be hard to remain hopeful about the promise of human nature when we read about private corporations buying up rights to sell drinking water at high prices to people who cannot possibly afford those prices. It is heartening, however, to learn of cases where the air and water and soil are being treated as a "commons," managed by democratically elected local governments (sometimes with private support) for the good of all.

The July 15/22, 2019 issue of *The Nation* has an article concerning President Trump's dumping desperate asylum seekers into America's cities and activists responding by providing aid and solidarity. The article ends with the example of a woman from Lutheran Social Services who spent hours one day cradling a sick child in her arms. The woman herself got very sick. "But instead of resenting the migrants for making her ill, she says fiercely, holding that baby "was the joy of my life." In such an event lives the promise of human nature.

The promise of human nature rests in our sense of the old values of reverence and love. We are caught up in the struggle between a materialist concept of self-interest and a natural way of democratic culture. Our hope is based on the realization that, like most animals, we humans have an innate capacity for empathy and a need to connect in community.

[1] Frances Moore Lappé and Anna Lappé, *Hope's Edge: The Next Diet for a Small Planet.* NY: Jeremy P. Tarcher\Putnam, 2002.
[2] Elliott Sober and David Sloan Wilson, *Unto Others.* Cambridge, MA: Harvard University Press, 1998, p. 336.
[3] "Why We're So Nice: We're Wired to Cooperate," by Natalie Angier. *The New York Times* Science section, 7/23/2002.

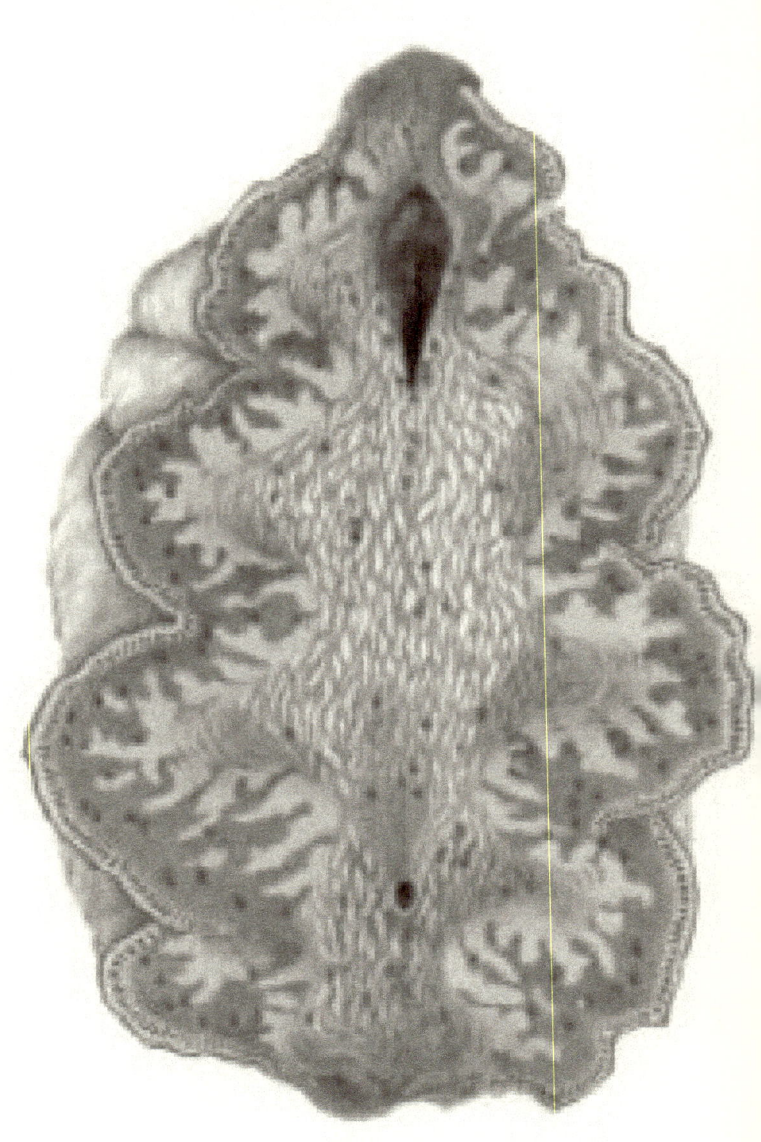

PART IV

GOD IN NATURE

We expand our view and place our considerations concerning human nature into the context of the cosmos.

"Our creator made all life, this we believe. Therefore, everything we see is a manifestation of this creation and demands our respect. All things that grow, walk, swim, and fly are our relatives, with purpose of being, and we are interdependent. We must be grateful and thankful for this abundance of life and spirit." ~*Chief Oren Lyons, Faithkeeper of the Onondaga Nation*

"Nature is the ultimate standard of reality, and from what has been revealed so far, I see the whole world as an organism with no truly separate parts." ~*Bernd Heinrich from* **Life Everlasting: The Animal Way of Death**

Chapter One

Cosmology and Creativity

The Necessity of Cosmology
The Universe as God's Creative Becoming

"What is below is like that which is above, and what is above is like that which is below, to accomplish the miracle of one thing." ~*Hermes Trismegistus*

"Maona (the Earth-Maker) is no personified deity to be seen with fleshly eye. He who would thus seek to look upon the Earth-Maker is but deceived by trivial things. Maona, to the Indian, is seen in all his works, and the whole world of nature tells of spiritual life. Maona is reflected in the mind of man himself, for man is like Maona when he has seen and understood Maona's works—the universe about him." ~*Natalie Curtis,* **The Indian's Book**

"We need a new creation story that connects us to nature and to others, one that can give us strength—that can make us real rather than rich. Nature, religions. and science coincide on the real: kinship with each other and with the mountains and prairies, oceans and forests." ~*Bernd Heinrich*

In his book, *The Life of the Cosmos*, physicist, Lee Smolin, writes of his belief ". . . in nature, in its dominance over us and in its recalcitrance to our fantasies and schemes."[1] He voices his concern over the extent to which the various social and scientific disciplines are divorced from contact with nature. His concern is shared by many thoughtful people of different religious persuasions. The question is, how may our social, scientific and religious outlooks be tied together in a way that reflects a healthy human relationship with nature?

Philosophy is, literally, "love of wisdom." But philosophers have differed concerning the scope of their subject. In modern times, the task of philosophy has usually either been reduced to an attempt to "dissolve" traditional philosophical problems by analyzing the language in which they have been framed ("conceptual analysis"), or its practitioners have taken a very different tack and focused on a psychological analysis of "the human condition" ("existentialism"). Both schools of thought share this: they assume that traditional attempts at metaphysics (the concern with the fundamental nature of reality) and its branch, cosmology (description of the natural order of the universe) have been proven a waste of time. They have concluded that cosmology is better left to scientists, or (God help us!) theologians.

Only a few modern philosophers have persisted in the traditional quest: to develop a coherent and adequate world view that takes the whole universe of human experience into account. Alfred North Whitehead and Charles Hartshorne were two of those increasingly rare modern "world view" philosophers who insist that it is the main business of philosophy to develop a cosmology and

NATURAL RELIGION

that the resulting world view be adequate, as well as consistent.

Any serious student of indigenous cultures cannot help but be impressed by the extent to which cosmology is essential to the Native's ways of life, how it provides a foundation for the manner in which they perceive themselves, for their rituals and ways of living. It is not overstating the case to assert that all significant cultures, from "primitive" to "civilized," define themselves in terms of the ways by which people perceive the cosmos. Such an awareness enables people to feel a direct connection to creation and to nature—or not, as their cosmology dictates.

If, as people have believed since the dawn of religion, cosmology provides a foundational model for life, and if cosmology reveals the connection we have with creation and nature, then whatever connection we feel or conceive of—whatever sense of a foundation we may have for our lives—is revealed in our cosmology. When we refuse the philosophical/theological task of conceiving a cosmology in the false belief that such a conception is too esoteric for our common interest, we pay the price of separation, of the loss of a sense of connection. Then we experience a void where a foundation ought to be.

If we are to get beyond the tired old arguments of the religion-verses-science debate, we shall need to confront some assumptions. The common religious view in our culture is that the universe is a material product of divine activity where the only question is whether God somehow intervenes now and then in an otherwise self-sustaining mechanism. An alternative view is that the universe—now said to be 13.7 billion years old—is somehow eternally self-existing. If not, a creator is implied. In addition, we have the currently popular scientific view that the universe emerged suddenly with a "big bang"(or "flaring forth," as Thomas Berry and Brian Swimme put it in *The Universe Story*) and the cause of that event is left as a mystery – or speculation, such as the idea of a "big bounce," the death of one universe leading to the birth of another. In each case, we are confronted with the question of how such a system can be self-sustaining (if not self-created) and also how such processes as thinking and feeling could ever have come about in a material universe.

The physicist, Lee Smolin speaks for many contemporary cosmologists when he writes: "We know enough to imagine how a universe like ours might have come to be without the infinite intelligence and foresight of a god. For is it not conceivable that the universe is as we find it because it made itself; because the order, structure and beauty we see reflected at every scale are the manifestations of a *continual process of self-organization, of self-tuning*, that has acted over very long periods of time?" Perhaps all this is ". . . evidence that the maker of the universe is nothing more or less than the random and statistical process of its own making."[2]

How could that be? The physical laws required for the exquisite "fine tuning" of the universe would seem to require an incredibly intelligent agent. Physicists agree that, at a very early stage in its development, the energy of the universe was balanced in such a way that if the whole thing had been even one billionth of a degree out of balance, it would all have either flown apart or imploded. Instead, the forces of gravity and of expansion were almost impossibly well- tuned. The chances of that having happened by some random or statistical process are very close to zero. How, then, are we to conceive of the universe without some supreme intelligence? What would be the nature of that intelligence?

In recent times, an old belief has re-emerged in a new guise: the holistic belief that the universe is a sort of organism *suffused with mind and feeling*. Holders of this belief tend to think of the universe as the body of God and see all existence as an expression of a divine impulse. The belief is that God desires self-expression and brings this about, ***not once with a "big bang," but continually***. It is also thought that God is involved directly in every aspect of the universe by means of a sort of thinking and a sort of feeling. The philosophical proponent of this point of view whom I have found persuasive is the Unitarian Universalist Charles Hartshorne who was influenced by Alfred North Whitehead among many others. I have found Hartshorne more comprehensible.

To say, as Deists do, that God is a Supreme Being who created the world but who did not remain directly involved, involves us in the supernaturalism of a theology that conceives of God as a great "watchmaker" who set the universe ticking and then withdrew, no doubt with amusement. To say that God *is* the physical creation—pantheism, as it is popularly conceived—leaves mind and feeling unintelligible and also fails to answer the question of causality. Those who say that God is a Supreme Mind (pure and simple) who is operative throughout the physical creation relegates physicality to an inferior status. This often accompanies a "superior" attitude, which regards bodily functions as debasements.

If it is in the nature of God to create, and creation is an

ongoing process—rather than a one-time event—then we may conceive of the universe as a dynamically evolving organism infused with God's feeling and mind. And yes, purpose. People who are put off by a belief in purpose in the universe present "an interesting object of study," as Whitehead put it. The purpose of materialists is to prove that there is no such thing as purpose in the universe! Or, as Charles Sanders Peirce put it, "Materialism is that mode of philosophizing which can be counted on to leave the world as unintelligible as it finds it."

Belief in the universe as a *divinely infused organism* is the foundation of animism. It is also the core perception of "process" philosophy and theology, of much current cosmological thinking, and of a *natural religion*. Classical theism conceives of God as an absolute spiritual being, set apart from creation, which, as we have seen, leads to all sorts of difficulties. One of them is the notion of Being as ultimate: essence before existence. Such a concept defies explanation. I think Hartshorne was correct when he wrote, "Today science and philosophy recognize none of the absolute worldly fixities the Greeks assumed—not the stars, not the species, not the atoms. It more and more appears that creative becoming is no secondary, deficient form of reality compared to being, but is, as Bergson says, 'reality itself.' Mere being is only an abstraction."[3] This philosophy holds that God is the all-inclusive reality, the Being of the universe. By this view, God is not *a separate* being; God is *the* one Being having a unique status, the one Subject upon whom all individual subjects depend. There is nothing apart from God.

There is an analogy that, I believe, takes us a long way toward understanding our place as part of the nature of this Being. I am puzzled not to have seen it discussed much. It is mentioned by Hartshorne. It is the analogy of our relationship to the cells of our own bodies. Our cells are individuals with whom we, as whole organisms, have a relationship. We could not exist without them, and yet we have individual identities that far exceed any of them in scope and complexity. Our cells feel, to some degree and also make choices, albeit in a manner that is very rudimentary in comparison with the choices we make. They are capable of either accepting or rejecting various kinds of nourishment or disease. Being so much more complex, our bodies (including, of course, our brains) would seem god-like to any of our cells, yet our cells are the means by which we both feel and think.

Your cells respond to your feelings and thoughts, and you respond to their feelings (and their thoughts—if they have any). Hurt them and you hurt yourself. Give them a healthy life and they respond with your sense of vitality. Your welfare and theirs is well-bonded. You have your own will and purposes for them, and they have a range of function over which you have no, or little, control. You can only hope to persuade them. If you love them and care for them, you are much better off than if you disdain them or ignore them. By your good will and thoughtful practice, you foster their well-being.

We are in the same sort of relationship with God as our cells are with us: God's mind permeates God's body, *the universe*. God, as an individual body and mind and range of feeling, is made up of an immense range of lesser individuals, all the way from electrons to the individuality of the totality. We exist somewhere in the middle of this vast range of creative being.

Creativity is the universal principle of all existence. Creativity exists within all the entities of creation. Creative process philosophy conceives of God as having an intimate, ongoing relationship with creation—which is closer to Biblical thinking than that of Christian theologians, who, like Aquinas, were much influenced by Greek philosophy. *Relationship*, not simple being, is a foundational principle of the universe. We may still ask, relationships of what? Are there no fundamental particles that obey some universal laws? The physicist, H.P. Stapp answered, that "An elementary particle is now an independently existing unanalyzable entity. It is, in essence, a set of relationships that reach outward to other things." And Werner Heisenberg: "The world . . . appears as a complicated tissue of events, in which connections of different kinds alternate or overlap or combine and thereby determine the texture of the whole." Relationships between events is also the process philosophy view.

An important part of conceiving of the universe as a gigantic creative organism, involves the notion of "center." *Where is the center of the universe?* Scientists have confirmed the wisdom of mystics like the Native American, Black Elk, who taught that the God of the Universe is a Center that is not located at any one point in space but is, rather, *everywhere*! We also live at the center of the omni-centric expansion of the universe.

We are presented with two seemingly conflicting discoveries: 1) that (in terms of the light from the beginning of time, first detected by Penzias and Wilson) the birthplace of the universe is 13.7 billion light-years away, and 2) that in terms of the expansion of galaxies

(Hubble's discovery), we are at the center of the universe, as is every single other thing! How can both be true? They are both true because there was no pre-existing space into which the universe expanded. The only "thing" that expands is the space between the particles. We are told to think about raisin bread expanding as it bakes: each raisin (galaxy) moves away from the other as the bread (space) expands. Each was originally at the center and remains a part of that center. So the universe is centered upon itself at each place of its existence.

Creation is not a one-time event; it is continuous. Cosmology now offers us a story of how the universe emerges ". . . out of all-nourishing abyss not only fifteen billion years ago but in every moment. Each instant, protons and antiprotons are flashing out of, and are as suddenly absorbed back into, all-nourishing abyss . . . a power that gives birth and that absorbs existence at a thing's annihilation. The foundational reality of the universe is this unseen ocean of potentiality."[4]

What about time? That's a question I have pondered for a long time! For me, the most persuasive treatment of time is that of the physicist Lee Smolin in his book, *Time Reborn*.[5] He calls the question, what is time? ". . . the single most important problem facing science," despite the fact that time is the most pervasive aspect of our everyday experience. Both physicists and philosophers have asserted—and many people think—that time is an illusion, that its real nature can be explained in terms of space, that, as Plato and Einstein taught, nothing really happens except a timeless rearrangement of particles in space and that there is no difference between past, present and future. They assert that whatever we may think of as real—truth, scientific laws, God—all exist outside of time. Smolin used to believe that, but he has come to the opposite conviction. Not only is time real, but nothing else gets as close to the heart of nature. Of course, this is a crucial practical issue as it relates to how we view our future and whether we may take the lessons of history seriously. Only if time is real may we see the future as open, not determined, and believe that our decisions have consequences.

The idea that everything moves in relation to everything else is fundamental to the idea that time moves in one direction, from past through present to future. As Smolin says, there are several ways of validating this assertion:

1. Cosmological – The universe is expanding.
2. Thermodynamic – Small things become more disordered in time.
3. Biological – People, other animals and plants are born, age, and die.
4. Experiential – We experience time flowing from past to future, remembering the past but not the future.
5. Electromagnetic – Light reaching our eyes gives us a view of the past but not the future as we measure long distances by the time it takes for the light to reach us from afar.

People have reconciled themselves to life's hardships and our mortality by believing in an eventual escape to a timeless spiritual world. But there is a price to be paid: a timeless world leaves no room for free will, decision-making, or any sort of freedom. It is the concept of freedom that Charles Hartshorne called the core of his philosophy.

Then there is evolution, a concept that depends upon time. The American philosopher, Charles Sanders Peirce, had a novel way of looking at reality. He said that only past events are real because they are established events that cannot be changed. The present is fleeting and the future is open, allowing for novelty – also uncertainty, a core principle of Buddhist philosophy. We live as parts of a universe that is highly structured and complex. That requires explanation, namely, a series of steps in sequence, the ordering of events in time.

The reality of time offers us a relational view that helps us see ourselves as interdependent individuals whose lives are made meaningful within a community relationship wherein people may care for one another.

A final practical consequence of taking time seriously is that it offers hope, even at this late date, that we shall be able to surmount the unprecedented and urgent problems raised by climate change. I trust my Epilogue offers some encouragement concerning what may be achieved when we put our minds and hearts to working in community.

Brian Swimme writes of some Indians in South America who teach that ". . . to become human 'one must make room in oneself for the immensities of the universe.' Unless we do so, we cannot find our true nature. We will wander in pain and loneliness . . . Caught in fragments of our nature, we will attach ourselves to one fragment after another, each taking us further away from our center."[6]

How can we view nature as the home for our spiritual growth when our spiritual contraction has combined with the fragmentation of a reductionist science to see nature as inert and valueless—other than as a commodity to be exploited? If only we may come to see that all things are connected in a manner that embodies a range of spiritual development, or of "subjectivity" as it is defined in this book, then we may be able to think, not only of ourselves, but of all beings in the world as being related in terms of a respectful sympathy.

[1] Lee Smolin, *The Life of the Cosmos*. NY: Oxford University Press, 1997, p. 296.
[2] Lee Smolin, p. 176.
[3] Charles Hartshorne, *Omnipotence and Other Theological Mistakes*. Albany: State University of New York, 1984.
[4] Brian Swimme, *The Hidden Heart of the Cosmos*. Orbis Books, Maryknoll, New York, 1996.
[5] Lee Smolin, *Time Reborn*. Mariner Books, Houghton Mifflin Harcourt, Boston, New York, 2013.
[6] Brian Swimme, p.108.

Chapter Two

Creative Evolution

*What are the principles underlying evolution?
Are present theories adequate?*

"To undergird the pluralistic global community that is aborning, we shall need . . . an expanded intellectual basis—a new way to think about origins, evolution, and the profound naturalness of life and its myriad patterns of unfolding."
~*Stuart Kauffman,* **At Home in the Universe**

The concept of evolution – constant change in nature - tells us more about reality than any other single point of view. It is the deepest of human ideas and the core of all physical, biological and social systems—*linking matter, life, and consciousness.* It explains how the universe has developed to the point of life on earth and how humans arose as an expression of the planet.

While our bodies show little in the way of intelligent design, they are amazingly well-suited for their environment. They are able to ward off disease, most of the time, and repair themselves when injured. As Chet Raymo put it, "Evolution by natural selection, for all of its jerry-rigged solutions, for all its failed experiments and blind alleys, is a wonderfully efficient way to populate a universe with diverse and interesting creatures."[1] The evolutionary process involves the development of genetic variations and natural selection of self-reproducing organisms.

Is that all there is to it? In order to answer this question, let us start with a remark of Albert Einstein who famously said that God does not play dice with the Universe. He wanted to believe in a universe where nothing is by chance, where everything is determined according to the eternally existing laws of physics.

The philosopher, Karl Popper, answered Einstein: "If God had wanted to put everything into the world from the beginning, He would have created a universe without change, without organisms and evolution, and without man and man's experience of change. But He seems to have thought that a live universe with events unexpected even by Himself would be more interesting than a dead one."[2] Popper suggested that God's knowledge of the future is limited—certainly not as limited as ours, but limited, nonetheless.

The Unitarian, Charles Darwin, also wanted to believe in a universe where God was fully in charge and didn't tolerate chance events that Darwin assumed would be meaningless. But his experience taught him that his belief was not well-founded. He was courageous enough to adjust his thinking to the evidence.

Darwin's discovery was the most far-reaching in history. He discovered that nature is not made complete and once and for all, but that *nature is in the process of making itself*, a work in progress. Many of us have become so accustomed to this idea that we now take it for granted. Even so, roughly half of the American population still believes in some form of creationism.

Even more devastating to believers in old-time religion than the idea of change is Darwin's discovery that change depends upon a process that involves chance. The geneticist, Jacques Monod said that chance ". . . is at the source of every innovation, of all creation in the biosphere."[3] As we shall see, that is an overstatement. But the point about chance is that it does not mean that mutations have no causes. Of course they do. But, whereas, a certain level of a certain sort of radiation or pollution might cause a certain percentage of mutations in some organisms, the actual mutation of a certain individual cell can still be accidental, a chance occurrence. It could just as easily have been another cell. The only thing that is caused is the probability that a certain percentage of cells will mutate. This is an important distinction because whether a certain individual cell mutates can have profound consequences. It can mean the difference between health or vitality and disease or deformity or even the evolution of a new species or not.

Without chance, there could be no freedom. If life were all determined (decreed by God in advance, or just in the nature of the material world) then notions of freedom or choice are meaningless. Chance implies freedom because it means that the world is not set up in a deterministic fashion. Things *do* just happen, accidentally, by chance.

Darwin was so shaken by his discovery of natural selection that he gave up believing in God because he assumed that both religion and science were committed to a philosophy of determinism, and that assumption left no room for chance and certainly none for purpose (other than God's). He argued correctly that the reality of evil was incompatible with a belief in a God conceived of as a great designer. Such a god would be a sadist. Let us not forget that the theology that Darwin undermined suggested that every monstrosity, every suffering, every birth of an unviable, ill-adapted animal was divinely decreed. Darwin found such an idea repugnant.

Darwin should have listened more to his friend, Kingsley, the English vicar and novelist, who wrote to him: "Now they have got rid of an interfering God—a master magician as I call it— they have to choose between the absolute empire of accident and a living, immanent, ever-working God."[4]

Charles Hartshorne took up that point when he wrote that to suppose that Darwinism reduces the origin of biological order to pure chance (Kingsley's "absolute empire of accident") is a mistake. For, as Hartshorne put it, ". . . there must be something positive limiting chance and something more than mere matter in matter, or Darwinism fails to explain life."[5]

Hartshorne's explanation took a new twist on the idea that the only positive explanation of order is the existence of an Orderer. Rather than the all-determining order of Greek philosophy and classical Christian theology, he went to the main point of evolution, which, since his writing, has become a mainstay of evolutionary thinking: *things tend to make themselves.* Creativity exists within all of the entities of creation. Creativity is a universal principle.

Evolution is not a puppet show being stage-managed by some divine being who made it all up for its own amusement. Life is much more interesting. As things evolve, they develop self-organizing capacities, which enable them to develop farther, to the point where they can change themselves and make others like themselves. They do this in the context of an amazingly complicated *web of relationships*.

The prevailing scientific view is that, at some stage of evolution, a mindless and feeling-less world gave rise to mind and feeling. An alternative view, held by process philosophers, and some scientists, insists on some manner of sensitivity all through the evolution of the universe. For Darwin, that included the cell, but nothing less complicated. For Hartshorne, as with Whitehead, the extent of sensitivity goes all the way to the so-called ultimate particles, which, in any case, no longer look like particles, but rather like a web of relationships.

No matter what view you take, it is obvious that the world of which we are a part is incredibly creative. As Brian Swimme and Thomas Berry put it in *The Universe Story*, "What is particularly striking is the lack of repetition in the developing universe . . . the extravagance of the creative outpouring, where each being is given its unique existence. At the heart of the universe is an outrageous bias for the novel, for the unfurling of surprise in prodigious dimensions throughout the vast range of existence. The creativity of each place and time differs from that of every other place and time."[6]

Berry and Swimme highlighted three principles at the root of the universe: differentiation, increased subjectivity, and communion. *Differentiation* enabled the universe to expand in a non-uniform manner, resulting in individual galactic and star systems. As evolution has proceeded, this principle has been made evident on earth by the extensive range of life-manifestations. The principle of increasing *subjectivity* is an important part of the view I am upholding. "From the shaping of the hydrogen atom to the formation of the human brain, interior psychic unity has consistently increased along with a greater complexification of being. This capacity for interiority involves increased unity of function through ever more complex organic structures . . . Earth becomes ever more subject to the free interplay of self-determining forces." A third principle of the universe—also emphasized in this book—is what Berry and Swimme call the *communion* of each of the entities in the universe. Science now confirms an old awareness, that we live in a universe wherein all things are connected, despite the immense space/time distances that might seem to rule out such communion.

Another principle made evident by the science of biology is *self-organization* and *self-regulation*. The only complete self that is organizing itself is the Universe as a whole. We are little bits of that self-organizing process. Even our whole earth is but a little bit of it.

We are beginning to understand how the principle of self-regulation unfolds in earth terms. The earth has maintained its ocean and atmosphere at pretty precise levels of salinity and average temperature for a long time despite some terribly traumatic events that, were it not for some self-regulating capacity, would have made our planet uninhabitable a long time ago. This improbable state of organized and regulated balance is accomplished solely by life itself as though the earth is, itself, an organism. This realization—of the earth as a self-organizing and self-regulating organism—has taken hold in terms of the *Gaia* concept, as suggested by James Lovelock.

An important example of the earth's self-regulation is

a well-functioning global communications network—not the recent human-invented Internet, but one that has been working on earth for billions of years: the planetary web of bacteria. The biologist Lynn Margulis has described how all of the world's bacteria have access to a single gene pool, and, therefore, to the adaptive mechanisms of the entire bacterial kingdom. The speed with which resistance spreads among bacterial communities is dramatic proof of the efficiency of their communications network. Margulis tells us that the different strains of bacteria can share hereditary traits and, typically, change up to 15% of their genetic material *on a daily basis*. All bacteria on this planet are part of a single microcosmic web of life. Technologies like genetic engineering and a global communications network, which we consider to be advanced achievements of our modern civilization, have been used by the planetary web of bacteria for billions of years, and they regulate life on Earth.

The creative principles I have mentioned combine to provide the answer to the Christian "creationists," who correctly point out that to get atoms in the universe to bounce together haphazardly to form a single molecule of an amino acid (the chemical building-block of living creatures)—that being a mechanistic version of Darwinian evolution—would require immensely more time than has existed. Yet amino acids have formed, not only on earth, but throughout the galaxy.

Even so there is no evidence that such a chemical wonder has occurred according to some design. Creationists are wrong when they insist that life as it is could have arisen only by means of the directive activity of God. They lack an understanding of evolutionary theory and the principle of self-organization. Yes, it is hard to conceive of how an amazing structure such as a primate's eye could have come about simply by chance, but we have ample evidence that our eyes are the result of a long process of evolutionary development as is the case with every organ in our bodies.

In preparation for this second edition, I read James A. Shapiro's book, *Evolution: A View from the 21st Century*.[8] Shapiro, Professor of microbiology at the University of Chicago, has been writing since 1992 about the importance of biologically regulated natural genetic engineering as a fundamental key concept in evolution science. This 2011 book provides evidence that cells and organisms sense their environment and transmit that information in their genomes. His new evolutionary synthesis reveals life to possess an immense subtlety of integration and "embedded sentience," that is to say, evidence of mindfulness!

Shapiro tells us how novelty arises in nature, innovation being the central issue here. He explains the many ways organisms actively change themselves, giving examples from the burgeoning science of genetics. His is the book to read if you want an authoritative view of the subject.

Living cells are not blind. "They continually acquire information about the external environment and monitor their internal operations. Then they use this information to guide the processes essential to survival, growth, and reproduction. Cells constantly adjust their metabolism to available nutrients, control their progress through the cell cycle to make sure that all progeny are complete at the time of division, repair damage as it occurs, and interact appropriately with other cells . . . they even undergo programmed cell death when suicide is beneficial to the entire population or to the multicellular organism as a whole" (p.7). All of that requires an elaborate sensory apparatus, the functioning of which ". . . requires cognition at all levels." In other words, life embodies decision-making capacities at even the cellular level.

Building on the work of his colleagues, Barbara McClintock and Lynn Margulis (among many others) Shapiro presents a view that is radically different from neo-Darwinian theory, as articulated by Francis Crick's famous Central Dogma of Molecular Biology. Using the ciliates as example of the ability of living cells to carry out biologically functional, rapid, and massive genome restructuring, he explains how such organisms ". . . reliably use thousands of DNA cleavage and resealing events to convert a meiotically functional genome into a structurally different somatic genome in a matter of several hours. Massive and rapid genome restructuring is occurring around us all the time" (p. 65).

Astounding as it may seem, we now have solid scientific evidence to back up the speculation of philosophers like Whitehead and Hartshorne that function-oriented, goal-seeking, capacities can be attributed to cells. Scientists have been trained to avoid that kind of teleological (goal-oriented) thinking at all costs. Yet here it is, backed up by experts in the field. "The idea of cellular cognition and decision-making with well-defined functional objectives has gone main-stream. Even Darwin entertained similar ideas, comparing the searching action of root tips to the operation of an animal brain" (p.137).

Differentiation, increased subjectivity, and communion are creative principles that form the basis for self-organization and self-regulation. Another creative principle, *spontaneity, is at work as cells make decisions*. Rupert Sheldrake wrote, "An inherent spontaneity in the life of nature has once again been recognized by science after a denial lasting over three hundred years. The future is not fully determined in advance; it is open. Insofar as it can be modeled mathematically, it has to be modeled in terms of chaotic dynamics. And this chaos, openness, spontaneity, and freedom of nature provide the matrix for evolutionary creativity."[9]

My first edition offered some "far out" speculation by scientists associated with the Santa Fe Institute concerning spontaneous self-organizing throughout the living—and even the non-living—world. For now, rather than getting bogged down in complexity theories, I am content to leave this subject with Shapiro's contemporary view. By this view, life, far from being an unlikely, but fortunate accident, is a natural expression of complex matter. Natural selection—the principle Darwin discovered—remains very important, of course, but ". . . has not labored alone to craft the fine architectures of the biosphere from cell to organism. Another source—self-organization—is the root source of order. The order of the biological world . . . is not merely tinkered, but arises naturally and spontaneously . . ."[10]

Not satisfied with theories of life that seem to leave out its aliveness, since the 1920s, some "holistic" or "organismic" theories have captivated the minds of an increasing number of scientists. Such theories stress the vitality of nature, even including crystals, molecules, and atoms. Some modern biologists have developed "field" theories based on the recognition that, as Rupert Sheldrake put it, ". . . living organisms have a wholeness that is more than the sum of the parts and their interactions. There is something within them that is holistic and purposive, directing them toward the normal adult form of their species . . ."[11] Shapiro, et al, would say that "something" is in the genetics. But where is the "aliveness?" By that, I mean the feeling, or, better, the emotion. My next chapter is an attempt to address the energy-field issue.

Notes to "Creative Evolution"

[1] Chet Raymo, "Intelligent design happens naturally," *Boston Globe*, 5/14/02.
[2] Karl Popper, quoted at the beginning of Charles Hartshorne, *Omnipotence and Other Theological Mistakes*. Albany: State University of New York, 1984.
[3] Jacques Monod, *Chance and Necessity*. London: Fontana/Collins, 1974, p. 69.
[4] Quoted by Charles Raven, *Natural Religion and Christian Theology. The Gifford Lectures*, 1951. First series. Science and Religion. Cambridge University Press.
[5] Charles Hartshorne, *The Logic of Perfection*. La Salle, IL: Open Court, 1967, p. 210.
[6] Thomas Berry and Brian Swimme, *The Universe Story*. San Francisco: Harper, 1992, p. 74.
[7] Thomas Berry, *The Dream of the Earth*. San Francisco: Sierra Club Books, 1988, p. 45.
[8] James A. Shapiro, *Evolution: A View from the 21st Century*. Upper Saddle River, NJ: Financial Times Science, 2011.
[9] Rupert Sheldrake, *The Rebirth of Nature*. NY: Bantam Books, 1991, p. 92.

[10] Stuart Kauffman, *At Home in the Universe.* New York: Oxford University Press, *1995, p. vii.*
[11] Sheldrake, p.107.

Chapter Three

Emotion Everywhere In a Conscious Cosmos

The aliveness of nature is primarily an emotional process, which includes a conscious component.

"If you study life deeply, its profundity will seize you suddenly with dizziness." ~*Albert Schweitzer*

"The energetic activity considered in physics is the emotional intensity entertained in life." ~*Alfred North Whitehead*

"Nature comes to us as constituted by feelings, not . . . mere lifeless, insentient matter." ~*Charles Hartshorne*

The realization that the aliveness of nature as a whole is primarily an emotional process is foundational for a natural religion. We have grown up in a world that is distorted by a philosophy of materialism, determinism, and the dualism that separates mind from matter—and us humans from a presumably unfeeling and unthinking nature. We have learned not to trust our own feelings in this regard, because feeling is presumed inferior to thought and because feeling has been considered a weakness. The idea that it is emotion and not thought that is primary, not only in us, but in the universe, may seem to be so outrageous, such a throwback to "primitiveness," that it is not worth considering. Yet, quantum physics, observant biology, and our own direct experience: all assign "emotion"— to a movement of energy that infuses a vast range of reality and that is also the basis of what we feel.

To say that the cells of animals or plants have no emotion would be to contradict what we can plainly observe. I shall not forget seeing the streaming of energy in elodea plant cells, as well as in amoeba, and the excitement I felt as I realized that even such a little bit of protoplasm ending its life under a microscope has surging within it the same basis of emotion as I do. It is a mistake to assume that, just because we can't live the life of a cell, such an individual entity has no feeling or ability to select between alternatives. Of course, we do live the lives of our cells in our bodies. They provide our physical being.

If the universe is the body of God, and emotion is prevalent in nature, then God is a very emotional being, who feels everything. The essential difference between the way God feels and the way you or I feel is that our feelings are limited to our experience; whereas God, who lives in the world by means of the experience of all entities, feels all experience.

Whether God or not, the basic relationship in reality is "feeling of another's feeling," as Hartshorne put it. I might say "resonance with another's emotion." In other words, sympathy. Sympathy is "an affinity, association, or relationship between persons or things wherein whatever affects one similarly affects the other" (*Webster's Dictionary*). Paired photons so behave! Their behavior indicates their instantaneous awareness of each other's energetic state, even when they are at such a distance from one another that it would take something traveling for some time at the speed of light to cover that distance! Physicists call that phenomenon "non-locality." Einstein called it "spooky action at a distance."

Whatever it may be—a human being, a cell within a human being, or a photon in outer space—if one entity is capable of having an effect on and being affected by another entity, there must be some sort of sympathetic resonance between them. Some scientists are convinced that *all* of the simplest, smallest entities in the universe are so connected: that they are all "aware" of one another and that the universe could not exist if they weren't.

Consciousness is based on feeling, which is based in emotion. The philosopher, C.S. Peirce, defined matter as "specialized and partially deadened mind." He wrote that protoplasm both feels and thinks. What is "mind?" If, as current cognitive thinking goes, mind is nothing but what brains do, then the word seems superfluous. Let us consider a functional definition: *mind is an ability to choose between alternatives;* choice is one of mind's characteristics. If that be the case, then mind might seem to be a rarity: there appears to be a lot more "programmed" responding than choosing going on in the natural world.

Nevertheless, a wide range of organisms certainly seem to make choices, even though some of them have no brains, or (in some cases) even nervous systems. The flatworm "Planaria" are brainless beings and can hardly be said to have nervous systems, yet they can be trained to learn how to select alternative routes, depending on the reward offered. The range of choice of a human cell certainly seems to be very small (compared with that of the human being as a whole), but how can we say that our cells live their entire lives without making any choices between alternatives when cells are observed to select or reject various potential food sources, pathogens, and so on. Saying that all such behavior is "purely instinctual" or "programmed" would seem to beg the question.

William Jordan spoke to this point in his beautiful book *A Cat Named Darwin* where he pointed out that living things without brains are still capable of responding appropriately to the world. Using the sugar maple as an example, he explains how it alters its physiology in order to enable it to survive the forces of winter. To him, this is an example of life being synonymous with intelligence. In this poignant book, Jordan explains how it is that a cat taught him to respect life and how we must first come to love life in order to respect it.

Obviously, the range of choice in nature must narrow nearly to the vanishing point as we go down the line to the simplest entities. Electrons are very much creatures of habit—but who is to say that electrons are immune of experience? The idea that all actualities have (or are) experiences might be rejected on the grounds that such things as rocks and hammers are, not only unconscious, but also show no sign of having any feeling. It seems true that a rock or a hammer, as a whole, has no experience, but this is not to say that the atoms or electrons in the rock or hammer have none. It is only to say that the rock or hammer is an example of a society of experiences that is organized in such a way that the inner experiences cancel each other out to produce a mere aggregation of effects. Experience may then be attributed to something if, and only if, it manifests the capacity to respond to things as a unified whole. The obvious duality in the world, between entities with a capacity for self-movement and those without such capacity, may then be explained in terms of organizational structure.

Some scientists have proposed that even atoms and molecules are "conscious," in the sense that they ". . . have the capacity to exchange information with each other and with their environment and to react to these in some quasi-intelligent fashion."[1] The founders of quantum physics struggled with the issue of the role of consciousness in physical theory. Despite their various interests and disagreements, each of them addressed the issue of the role of consciousness in the establishment of physical reality.

The physicist, Erwin Schrodinger (who was also a student of Eastern and Western mysticism) interpreted the findings of quantum physics as a breaking of the barrier that Western culture has erected between mind and the physical world: "Consciousness is that by which this world first becomes manifest, by which, indeed, we can quite calmly say, it first becomes present; that the world *consists* of the elements of consciousness.[2] And "Mind has erected the objective outside world of the natural philosopher out of its own stuff."[3]

Following the thinking of Schrodinger, De Broglie and other prominent physicists, Princeton scientists Robert G. Jahn and Brenda J. Dunne, have summed up this point of view: "Physical theory cannot be complete until consciousness is somehow acknowledged as an active element in the establishment of reality."[4] In chapters called "Consciousness Atoms" and "The Waves of Consciousness" they represent consciousness in terms of "probability-of-experience waves," that ". . . range freely over their own space-time domains, somewhat like the physical waves that ride the open ocean surface or those that propagate sound or light over large unbounded regions."[5]

However, Jahn and Dunne remind us that the fundamental ". . . wave/particle paradoxes of physics have not been fully resolved in any convincing philosophical sense." They point out that ". . . it is not the physical world per se that imposes such dichotomy; it is our consciousness. More precisely, it is imposed by the process of consciousness interacting with its physical environment."

They take hope from this dilemma: "And if this interpretation is valid, then it is also consistent to attribute to consciousness itself the option of wave-like as well as particulate behavior, again as perceived by that same consciousness."[6]

"The universe shivers with wonder in the depths of the human."[7] It is wonderful that we are beings in whom the universe has become conscious of itself—although almost certainly not the only ones. Some form of intelligent reflection on itself was implicit in the universe from the beginning. This is now recognized by many scientists. But this realization is still not generally appreciated. This is because we are still largely confined emotionally, unable to resonate with the world around us. For the most part, we humans remain oblivious to our cosmic connection.

[1]Jahn and Dunne, *Margins of Reality*, San Diego: Harcourt Brace, 1987, p. 317bf.
[2]Erwin Schrodinger, *My View of the World* (Cambridge: The University Press, 1964), p. 137.
[3]Schrodinger, "Mind and Matter," in *What Is Life? and Mind and Matter* (Cambridge: The University Press, 1967), p. 131.
[4]Jahn and Dunne, p. 61.
[5]Jahn and Dunne, p. 242.
[6]Jahn and Dunne, p. 211.
[7]Brian Swimme, quoted by Thomas Berry in *The Dream of the Earth*, San Francisco: Sierra Club Books, 1988, p. 16.

Chapter Four

A Field for Emotion and Thought

What ties it all together... The "ether," "chi," "orgone," "Zero-point Field" is as real as you are.

"The evident ability of electromagnetic waves to propagate through a vacuum raises difficult questions about the properties of a total void that can support the oscillating stresses of the alternating electric and magnetic fields. Search for characteristics of this 'ether' has occupied physicists for over a century, and the issue remains incompletely resolved." ~*Robert G. Jahn and Brenda J. Dunne,* **Margins of Reality** *(1987)*

"All things, material and spiritual, originate from one source and are related as if they were one family. The past, present, and future are all contained in the life force." ~*Morihei Ueshiba*

Scientists have identified a nonmaterial realm that permeates the entire universe, including every living being. This meeting place of the nonmaterial and material realm is a point where science and religion have something in common: the attempt to understand the universe as unified and full of subjectivity, emotion and mind.

Albert Einstein is well known for the theory that got rid of the "ether," the invisible energy field that was thought to permeate the universe. The famous Mickelson-Morely experiment, believed to prove him right, has been duplicated to the satisfaction of most scientists. But that experiment is based on an important assumption: that the "ether" is stationary—it just sits there and doesn't itself move. What if the ether moves of its own? What if the ether is a massless energy that permeates all matter and even all space? What if there is an all-pervasive energy-field that makes all life, all existence, possible?

In order to answer this question, let us first consider "dark matter." The physicist, George Smoot, wrote: "The gossamer network of galaxies we see in the night sky is the shimmering dew on a cosmic cobweb, as visible matter outlines the shape of structures of invisible dark matter, to which it has been drawn by gravitational attraction."[1] Dark matter cannot be seen by any scientific instrument but is assumed to exist because of the behavior of measurable matter in its presumed presence.

Also, we may read about a subatomic particle called the Higgs Boson. By the time of the writing of this second edition, the Higgs Boson has been verified as the explanation of the origin of mass; that is, it gives particles mass. The Higgs particle, like all particles, may also be thought of as a field that permeates all space. Before the Higgs field "kicked in," the universe was just space and massless subatomic particles. After the Higgs field gave everything mass, the particles clumped together and formed atoms, stars, bugs, and, eventually, you.

As if all of the above weren't enough to ponder, we

also have "dark energy" to contend with. Astronomers have calculated from NASA data that only 4% of the universe is made up of atoms with known forces such as electromagnetism and gravity. 23% is "dark matter." And the remainder—73%—is made up of yet another poorly understood force called "dark energy."

What I find interesting about the Higgs field and dark energy is that these concepts represent something more than efforts in search of entities implied by current theories. They are also attempts to understand something that has been assumed for a long time: a fundamental, spontaneous, moving energy field that connects everything and that is the basis of all life. Religions all have a name for it. And practitioners of most of the martial arts depend on it, as do those of acupuncture and some other healing arts.

In the mid-1900s, the biologist Frank A. Brown at Northwestern University was doing research on the relationship of the bio-cycles of living organisms to the earth's electromagnetic field. Harold S. Burr, at Yale University, was investigating the electromagnetic fields around living organisms. The orthopedic surgeon, Dr. Robert O. Becker, was making important discoveries regarding regeneration of damaged or lost tissue in various animals, including the human. His research regarding the unhealthy effects of electromagnetic waves generated by electric power lines and ordinary household appliances was discouraged by the power industries.

Lynne McTaggart's book, *The Field*, reported on the work of these and others of a growing group of scientists with impressive credentials who have contributed to our understanding of the all-pervasive energy-field of the universe. Among many others, they include Brenda Dunne and Robert Jahn of the Princeton Engineering Anomalies Research group; Fritz-Albert Popp, theoretical physicist; Karl Pribram, neuroscientist; Hal Puthoff, laser physicist; and William Tiller, of the Stanford Research Institute.

A brief summary of their findings goes something like this: quantum physics had determined that subatomic particles had no meaning in isolation, but only in relationship with everything else. It had been a mistake to think of material things as composed of self-contained little atoms. The reality of matter is that its totality is indivisible, except by human effort. The whole universe is a dynamic web of interconnection. Once in contact, all "particles" remain so—indeed, have always been so. The question is: what serves as the linking force, the "tying together" of such connection? Without some sort of "carrier" of such "influence," we are reduced to Einstein's dreaded "spooky action at a distance."

It gets really weird when we are told that the smallest bits of matter exist in all possible states until they are "disturbed" by our observing them, at which point they "settle down" into something "real"—at least to us. It turns out that our human consciousness is presumed essential to this subatomic "flux" turning into some set "thing." But the physicists had no way to factor this consciousness into their equations, and so their theories lacked coherence.

Lynne McTaggart noted a crucial development: "A small band of scientists dotted around the globe . . . thought again about a few equations that had always been subtracted out in quantum physics. These equations stood for the Zero Point Field—an ocean of microscopic vibrations in the space between things. If the Zero Point Field were included in our conception of the most fundamental nature of matter, they realized, the very underpinning of our universe was a heaving sea of energy—one vast quantum field. If this were true, everything would be connected to everything else like some invisible web . . . Most fundamentally, they had provided evidence that all of us connect with each other and the world at the very undercoat of our being. Through scientific experiment they'd demonstrated that there may be such a thing as a life force flowing through the universe—what has variously been called collective consciousness or, as theologians have termed it, the Holy Spirit . . . They offered us, in a sense, a science of religion."[2]

According to this "new discovery," there is no such thing as empty space. The "vacuum" is actually a "hive of activity," a "seething maelstrom" of subatomic particles popping in and out of existence. The energy involved in this very brief creation and destruction dance is enormous, more than is contained in all of the matter in the world. It has been calculated that the total energy of this "field of all fields" exceeds all energy in matter by a factor of ten to the fortieth power! The physicist, Richard Feynman, said that the energy in a cubic meter of "empty" space is enough to boil all the oceans of the world. No wonder that some physicists are trying to figure out how to tap into this inexhaustible "dark" energy.

So the "ether" has returned to physics as scientists have concluded that a strange "dark energy" fills the universe and makes up 73% of its reality. This invisible energy exists everywhere, even in vacuums. "The case for dark energy has been building brick by brick for nearly a decade," say Princeton University professors Jeremiah P. Ostriker and Paul J. Steinhardt in an article in *Scientific American*. They explain how this mysterious energy is a discovery of the highest magnitude. Indeed, they admit, " . . . we have been missing most of the story." (3)

If, as seems to be the case, all of the matter in the universe is tied together by an underlying field of energy, we have a scientific validation and explanation for much human experience that has been interpreted in religious terms. People were wrong to think that the universe is composed of isolated bits of matter, operating by means of blind and mechanistic processes. The real universe is rather a ". . . vast dynamic web of energy exchange, with a substructure containing all possible versions of all possible forms of matter. Nature is not blind and mechanistic, but open-ended, intelligent and purposeful, making use of a cohesive learning feedback process of information being fed back and forth between organisms and their environment." Its unifying mechanism: the encoding and transmission of all the information in the universe— everywhere and at once![4]

Some of today's scientists see the mysterious-seeming relationship between our consciousness and the world of matter in these terms: The Field, rather than any chemical reaction, ". . . is responsible for our mind's highest functions" and is ". . . the force, rather than germs or genes, that finally determines whether we are healthy or ill, the force that must be tapped in order to heal. We are attached and engaged, indivisible from our world, and our only fundamental truth is our relationship with it."[5]

Belief in the existence of "The Field" has been at the heart of religious thinking and practice since the dawn of humankind. Every religion has a name for it. In India it is called *prana*; in China, *chi*; in Japan, *ki*; in Judaism, *ruach* (wind, breath, spirit); in Christianity, *Holy Spirit*; in Native American religion, *Great Spirit*. For many of those cultures, the idea of "life force" is, or was, central to their martial and healing arts. For example, a martial arts master, B.K. Frantzis, who also has over 30 years of experience in Oriental healing arts, writes, "Whereas the external arts develop the bones, muscles, and outer physique, the internal arts concentrate on the development of chi . . . so that chi becomes as tangible as a solid object. The energy field in the air becomes as real to a Chi Gong or internal art practitioner as the water in the ocean is to a swimmer."[5]

Developing chi energy is the focus of Taoism, China's original religion/philosophy. As with Wilhelm Reich's therapy, the practice involves clearing away energy blocks in the body, so that energy can stream freely. Reich's therapy often includes physical pressure on knotted muscles; Chi Gong concentrates on simple awareness and application of the power of the mind to clear energy blocks in the body. As with Aikido (at least as some of us practice it), "Chi Gong works with the muscles quite differently than typical exercises do. Aerobics and vigorous stretching build strength and flexibility; Chi Gong and other internal exercises build effortless power and looseness . . . In the internal arts, the feeling of strength is considered inappropriate; the goal, rather, is a feeling of relaxed power. Relaxed power comes when the muscles, rather than fighting and straining to do something, just loosen (open up) and allow the energy to flow through."[6] I remember an Aikido session *led by a master from Japan who needed a translator. At one point, we sat as he went on for what seemed a long time. Translation: "He says to relax."* How true. Aikido goes much better that way.

Most of the martial arts are founded on an understanding of how this mysterious chi or ki force can actually be found within oneself and increased to produce amazing results. The "unbendable arm" exercise in Aikido is a good example of "allowing the energy to flow through." At an Aikido workshop, I saw a physicist declare that it was physically impossible to resist having one's arm pulled down without using muscle power—until he learned how to do it for himself. He was amazed. He said, "There is nothing in physics that can explain this."

Wilhelm Reich was ridiculed and vilified and even imprisoned for his insistence that he had discovered "orgone" energy. His books were burned in the United States of America in the 1950s because they were all said to be promoting his "fraudulent" orgone energy accumulator, with respect to which he was said to have made outlandish claims. The Food and Drug Administration had the accumulator "tested." They refused to let Reich explain how to go about the testing. They knew better. They had some dying cancer patients sit in it. The result was that the patients' health deteriorated faster than expected. The scientists concluded that the accumulator was fraudulent because it "had no effect!" They hadn't asked the obvious question: *why did the patients get worse sooner than expected?* Had he been given the chance, Reich would have explained it. The testing was done next to a room where there was an X-ray machine in almost constant use. Reich would have told them that X-ray radiation is deadly to orgone energy. But they wouldn't have believed him.[7] Many people have claimed beneficial effects of the accumulator. In their efforts to put Reich in jail, the FDA representatives were unable to find a single user who was willing to testify against him.

I built a small accumulator and a control box, in order to see if I could duplicate Reich's experiments regarding heat production by the accumulation of orgone energy. My results were essentially the same as his, even to the point of changes due to barometric pressure. The accumulator was a good weather predictor. I asked a physicist friend for his view of my little accumulator. Before many words were out of my mouth, he had an explanation: air convection. I showed how I had controlled for that. Well, then, *it must be black body radiation*. But he was unable to explain how black body radiation served the purpose; clearly, it was just his guess. And he quickly lost interest. This is the sort of experience that Reich and his students had had for many years and that has taught me that "it must be___" is not a legitimate scientific statement.

Reich met with Albert Einstein for nearly five hours on January 13, 1941, during which time Reich showed Einstein some of his experiments with orgone energy. The only detailed report of that meeting is that of Reich's. His detractors simply say that Einstein was polite on the surface, all the while thinking that Reich was a quack. They do not seem to realize that such duplicity does not speak well for Einstein. This much is clear: Einstein abruptly broke off contact with Reich, after promising to repeat the experiments they had done together. Foreseeing some difficulty, Reich asked Einstein to promise that, in case of doubt, he would continue the conversation. Instead, Einstein wrote to Reich, saying that his "assistant" had explained-away Reich's demonstrations of orgone energy to Einstein's satisfaction and there was no need for further discussion. Reich's rebuttal of the assistant's explanation and attempt to continue the conversation was met with silence. (See Jerome Eden, M.A., "The Einstein Affair," *The Journal of Orgonomy*, Vol. 5, No. 2, Nov., 1971.)

Though not convinced of all things orgonomic, I have always respected Wilhelm Reich, not only for his generally accepted contributions to character analysis in the early days of his association with psychoanalysis, but—and this is much more important—for the fact that he was one of those rare individuals in modern times who was able to have contact with the streaming of energy in the body (his own and those of his patients) and not run from it. This streaming is literally the most natural thing in the world, and yet, for armored individuals—and, truth to tell, most of us are armored—it is the most frightening, to the point where people will resort to all manner of evasive, if not sadistic and masochistic behaviors in order to avoid the streaming—or keep it under control.

I have had a lot of therapy with four different practitioners of the therapy Reich taught, and I am very grateful for those experiences. They included many instances where I felt the streaming. One time, the energy welled up in my center, which was very frightening, and then flowed throughout my body, which became rigid until the energy was released. I must have looked like someone having a seizure. I had no control over the experience. What a scary business, for a twentieth century white American male to have no control over his feelings! Well worth it, though. With this "breaking of the diaphragmatic block," I was free to breathe more fully than I had since I was very young.

If you want to see what Orgone therapy looks like—it is not the same for any two people, but there are important similarities—I recommend the film, *Room for Happiness*, produced by The College of Orgonomy, P.O. Box 490, Princeton, New Jersey 08542. Email: aco@orgonomy.org

If you want to learn more about Orgone biophysics or any other aspect of Orgonomy, The College of Orgonomy has a list of books—including Myron Sharaf's definitive biography of Reich. Also, in 2015, Professor James E. Strick, chair of the Program in Science, Technology and Society at Franklin and Marshall College, published a big book, *Wilhelm Reich, Biologist* (Harvard University Press) in which he shows how, contrary to the dominant disparaging narrative, at least during 1934-1939, Reich was doing careful, state-of-the-art research in laboratory biology. (It should go without saying that I speak only for myself and make no claim to represent Orgonomy.)

After my "breakthrough" experience (noted above), I thought of John 7:38: "He who believes in me, as the scripture has said, 'Out of his middle ("belly" and "heart" are two common translations) shall flow rivers of living water.'" The gospel author interprets: "Now this he said about the Spirit." There being no mention of any such thing in the Hebrew Bible, we must go to certain Essene documents for Jesus' scriptural reference. Jesus was clearly a healer as were some of the Essenes. The large sign of the cross, used in early Christian times, points to some of the segments wherein energy gets blocked according to Reich, and according to the Hindu "chakra" system.

Jesus taught that, to enter the Kingdom of Heaven, we must "become as a child." It is a fundamental Taoist proposition that we must make our bodies childlike, since, before armoring, children's bodies are wonderfully efficient. They have big bellies and supple chests. For their size, they are much stronger and more filled with energy than adults. Try imitating the sounds and movements of a young child. You won't be able to keep up for long. She'll outlast you by a long shot! Children and animals have this in common: both breathe from the belly and have relaxed chests. The internal organs are massaged by every breath, which makes the body healthy and strong.

Most of us believe most of what we believe because of what we've heard or read. Few will take the trouble to find out for themselves. Of course, it is possible to fool oneself, but I have come to trust my own experience over what someone else says ought to be my experience. I recommend that attitude to the readers of this book.

So what enables photons, electrons, atoms, cells, minds, and feeling-states to communicate, resonate, influence, or have sympathy with one another? The answer has been sensed for a long time and is now better understood in scientific terms. We keep running up against terms like "influence" and "resonate." Does the chi/ki/orgone energy of The Field serve as the medium through which feeling and thought moves beyond the brain? Since this energy is not stationary but moves spontaneously, it may be that here we have a good, natural explanation for psychic phenomena such as telepathic communication and other parapsychological effects.

We will consider another important function of The Field in Chapter Seven. But first, I'd like for the reader to join me in pondering the power of God.

[1] George Smoot (and Keay Davidson), *Wrinkles in Time*. NY: Avon Books, 1993, p. 286.
[2] Lynne McTaggart, *The Field*. New York: Harper/Collins, 2002, p. xviif.
[3] "Quintessential Universe," Ostriker & Steinhardt, *Scientific American*, January, 2001.
[4] McTaggert, p. 95.
[5] B.K. Frantzis, *Opening the Energy Gates of Your Body*. Berkley: North Atlantic Books, 1993, p. xxii.
[6] Frantzis, p. 11.
[7] "An Analysis of the United States Food and Drug Administration's Scientific Evidence Against Wilhelm Reich," by Richard A. Blasband, M.D., C. Fredrick Rosenblum, B.S., and David Blasband, LL.D., *The Journal of Orgonomy*, Vol. 6, No. 2, Nov., 1972.

Chapter Five

Pondering the Power of God

God's power is not tyrannical, but appealing and persuasive—and therefore responsible.

"We do not honor God by breaking down the human soul, connecting it with him only by a tie of slavish dependence. It is his glory that he creates beings like himself, free beings . . . that he confers on them the reality, not the show, of power."
~*William Ellery Channing (1788-1842)*

In 1894 a town in Spain published a resolution: "Considering that the Supreme Creator has not behaved well in this province, as in the whole of last year only one shower of rain fell; that in this summer, notwithstanding all the processions, prayers and praises, it has not rained at all, and consequently [our] crops . . . are entirely ruined, it is decreed:

"Article 1. If within the peremptory period of eight days from the date of this decree rain does not fall abundantly, no one will go to mass or say prayers.

"Article 2. If the drought continues eight days more, the churches and chapels shall be burned, and missals, rosaries, and other objects of devotion will be destroyed.

"Article 3. If, finally, in a third period of eight days it shall not rain, all priests, friars, nuns, and saints, male and female, will be beheaded. And for the present, permission is given for the commission of all sorts of sin, in order that the Supreme Creator may understand with whom he has to deal." Ho, ho!

It is said that, four days after this proclamation was made, the heaviest rainfall known for years was precipitated upon the community. Causal connection? Chance event? Any purpose involved?

Religions that hold that the world was created by a divine reality (usually said to exert ongoing influence in the world) have also usually insisted that God is different in kind from worldly entities, with a sort of causal power that differs in kind from all creatures. Trying to buttress their faith, theologians of the Dark and Middle Ages got into Greek philosophy and wound up reasoning that, since God is perfect in power and knowledge, whatever happens is divinely made to happen and has already been known to God—that, since God knows all our thoughts and actions in advance, they have already been decided.

We need a rational alternative to the idea that God's power is that of a despot who has to control everything. We do not live in that sort of universe. If we are to have a belief in God at all, the reasonable alternative is that God's power is the universal creativity, which makes room for human freedom, a balance of choice and chance and cause and effect—and will and purpose. We are a part of that process.

The central idea is that of creativity, which assumes the existence of beings that exercise free will. This idea of freedom is upheld in the philosophies of William James, Henri Bergson, Charles Sanders Peirce, Alfred North Whitehead, and Charles Hartshorne—to name the most persuasive advocates in modern times. As Hartshorne noted, an early proponent was a theologian who has been called the first Unitarian: Socinus, who attributed to Jesus a divine mission but did not worship him. Like modern Unitarians, Socinus was sympathetic with the science of his time. Along with their rejection of a tyrant deity, Socinus and his followers also rejected the standard definition of God as "unmoved mover" and first cause of all things, entirely independent of the world. Instead, they held that God was actually influenced by the events of the world. This belief resonates with Biblical philosophy, which, in general teaches that God knows what we do, but not eternally or beforehand. God does not determine our acts; we do. And when we do, God gains knowledge made possible by our doing. Rather than our lives being of no lasting consequence, we produce effects in the everlasting life of God.

The earliest Unitarians revised radically the philosophical fundamentals of Christian religion. They did so because they believed in freedom and creativity. The most important spokesperson for Unitarianism in 19th century America, William Ellery Channing, was a staunch advocate of their point of view concerning the nature of God and human freedom.

Another non-Trinitarian version of Christianity, Universalism, also broke with tradition by rejecting the doctrine of eternal punishment. Unlike the traditional Universalists, contemporary process theologians also reject the idea of heavenly rewards.

We are mortal. Only God is immortal. God's power in the world is not that of a tyrant, but that of a responsible divine love. It is the power of appeal and persuasion, not command and coercion. The Source of our freedom cannot force us to do anything.

God knows everything there is to know—and no more. What can be known about the future is that it is open, a range of possibilities and probabilities. Nothing is fixed or settled. God shares the adventure of time with us. There has always been a world in which God has been creatively active, because it is God's nature to be creative.

God is everywhere, at all times. But our experience of God is so interwoven with the world that we see God only "through a glass, darkly." Revelation, though omnipresent, is (usually) ambiguous. I think of Robert Frost's poem about seeing some flowers from a moving train. "Heaven gives its glimpses only to those who are not in a position to look too close."

Whitehead and Hartshorne taught that the principle that *there is no entity that requires nothing but itself to exist* applies even to God. This means that God requires the (or at least a) world to exist as much as the world requires God—because it is of the nature of God to create. At the root of the necessities belonging to the nature of the God-world relation is creativity, the process whereby each event of the world arises out of the many past events, exercises some degree of self-determination, and then exerts influence upon the totality of future events. If this basic casual principle is truly metaphysical and doesn't just belong to a contingent creation, it cannot be interrupted by God: it *must* characterize the interactions between God and the world.

God, according to this view, shares this characteristic with the world: like us, God is "a personally ordered society of occasions of experience." If so, God—the soul of the universe—is *both* immanent and transcendent. God is immanent in the sense that *the very nature of God is to be related to the world.* God is part of, rather than outside, the process of creation. God is involved in all worldly events. But God is a (the only) special case, being also transcendent: beyond any finite cosmic epoch.

This philosophy offers us a very different notion of divine power from that of an omnipotent being, ruling the world from without. God sustains the world *from within* by means of the power of creativity. Progress involves the development of creatures with ever-greater capacity for depth and intensity of experience. Complex social order is a means toward more novel forms of creativity.

Each individual entity in creation has some degree of freedom to respond or not to respond to the divine influence. That degree of freedom must be nearly nonexistent at the level of electrons, which are obviously very habitual creatures, but it is highly significant at the level of the human being.

This concept is that of a responsible god. As Hartshorne put it, "A wholly absolute god is power divorced from responsiveness or sensitivity; a power which is not responsive is irresponsible."[1] God's power is a way of responsibility: persuasive, but not compelling.

How are we to believe in a responsive and responsible God, knowing of so much evil in the world?

---

[1] Charles Hartshorne, *The Divine Relativity: A Social Conception of God.* The Terry Lectures, 1947. New Haven: Yale University Press, 1948, p. 164.

Chapter Six

The Problem of Evil

God feels our feelings and treats us as adults.

"The traditional doctrines of theology do not solve the painful problem of evil. The ordinary conception of the creation of the world and the Fall turns it all into a divine comedy, a play that God plays with himself." ~*Nikolai Berdyaev (1874-1948)*

"What a terrifying marvel: man deliberates, and God awaits his decision! God, who sees things change, changes also in beholding them." ~*Jules Lequier (1814-1862)*

"Men never do evil so completely and cheerfully as when they do it from religious conviction." ~*Blaise Pascal*

Since September 11, 2001, lovers of liberty everywhere have confronted the problem of evil with a renewed sense of urgency. Why do bad things happen to innocent people?

Various religious answers have been provided. Like Zoroaster, the 2nd century Christian heretic, Marcion, suggested there were two gods: a supreme God of love and an inferior God who allows violence, sickness and pain. He was not able to deal well with the question of the God-of-love's supremacy in such a set-up.

Theologians have wrestled with the issue for a long time. Many have said that God allows evil as retribution for the original sin, but their attempts to explain why a good God would punish all humanity for one man's disobedience amount to justifying a divine tyranny. A related approach has been to blame the devil, but holders of that view have never explained why God allowed Satan to possess such power. Over half of Americans believe that the Devil exists, and some blame Satan for feminism, famine in Africa, and the homosexual rights movement.

For many people, the problem of evil is resolved by unquestioning faith in the goodness of a God whose actions are inscrutable. I have discussed the inadequacy of such a view. This problem did not exist before the rise of monotheism. In earlier times, the world was believed to be more or less controlled by a multitude of gods and goddesses, some benevolent, some mischievous—much like human beings. The only issue then was the practical one of either getting in the good graces of the gods or of trying to influence their behavior.

While those same issues persisted in monotheism, an ethical element was added: how do we know when we're doing God's will? And dare we ask whether God's will is good—in the light of so much evil in the world? Many have attempted to explain how a good God can permit all of the bad things that happen to people or that people inflict on each other.

If we are to believe in God, the only such conviction that makes ethical sense is to tie it in with the sort of God described in this book, the God of Creativity. Creativity implies freedom, the freedom to create. If God is to create by means of creative creatures, those individuals must have the freedom to make decisions. As Charles Hartshorne succinctly put it: "The root of evil, suffering, misfortune, wickedness, is the same as the root of all good, joy, happiness, and that is freedom, decision-making."[1]

How could it be otherwise, if creativity is to have any meaning? There can be no such thing as a moral action without the freedom to decide for or against it; therefore, evil, as well as good, is always an option.

Does science throw any light on the problem of evil? Yes, especially the theory of evolution. The basic principle is simple: violence and death—especially, the predator-prey arrangement— are necessary conditions for the existence of life. Joseph Campbell used to say that a lot of mythology may be understood once we accept the reality that life feeds on life. If natural forces were not aggressive, conscious creatures could never have evolved.

A fundamental principle of life is the persistence of species. We change our atoms and cells many times during our lifetimes, but the information encoded in our genes and stored in our memories lives on. To do so, we must take energy from our environment. As life proliferates on the finite surface of the planet, competition for resources inevitably ensues. Aggression becomes necessary for survival and the propagation of species. Like malaria pathogens and AIDS viruses, we kill and consume other species in order to endure.

There is no moral dimension to the story of predators and prey or parasites that kill in the natural world. Malaria kills more than a million people a year without the plasmodium or its mosquito host bearing us any grudge. Like us, those individuals are just making their living. The ethical issue arises when we are able to contemplate our human role with respect to measures that can prevent people from the infection or from dying due to a weakened immune system.

It has often been asserted that we humans are the only moral species, but that is not the case. The moral behavior of many other species is actually superior to ours. Humans constitute one of the few species that wars on its own kind. There are many other species who exhibit cooperative behaviors based on decision-making. But we are the most significant moral species because we have, by far, the most power to make lasting changes in the world. With power comes responsibility, and ours is immense.

Violence in nature has a creative side: competition for resources results in variations that drive life toward greater complexity, even to consciousness. It is this consciousness that offers us a means of escape from the relentless logic of biological necessity. Our genes may predispose us to act in certain ways, but they do not constrain us. We have some capacity to choose good over evil. The ethical issue is: how do we create a cooperative human society living in harmony with the earth?

You may still wonder about God's role, if any, regarding the problem of evil. It boils down to this question: does God care for us; and if so, how does this caring manifest itself? No one can care without feeling something, not even God. But most philosophers and theologians have rejected feeling as a divine attribute. For them, feeling has meant weakness. Only a few have been able to see that any divine knowledge of our feelings is, itself, a manner of feeling.

Like A. N. Whitehead, Charles Hartshorne saw the mind of God as being so mixed in with the energy/matter of creation that that mind actually feels the feelings of all the subjects of the universe. We are talking about ". . . not mere benevolence that constitutes the divine nature, but love in the proper sense. Cruelty to other creatures, or to oneself, means contributing to vicarious divine suffering. Hence, of course we should love our fellows as we love ourselves, for the final significance of their joy or sorrow is the same as the final significance of our joy or sorrow, that they will be felt by God."[2]

If this is so, then God cares for us, and not merely because of a unique brief time of suffering (Jesus), but by means of direct sympathy, at all times and places. That is a divine love to which we can relate, if we are aware of it, and to which we are related whether aware of it or not.

We are not set apart as some special creation: we are part of an incredibly immense web of existence that has at its basis something akin to the feelings we feel. We are not strangers living alone in an alien universe. We are always at home.

Christian teaching holds the belief that when we cause suffering or adds joy to another person, Christ suffers or is joyful. "Insofar as you did it to the least of these, you did it to me." The concept of Christ is meant to provide a link between God and us. What if we don't need such a mythological link? What if we are already connected in such a way that the bond is inescapable? Then God really is love, *and in the only sense in which love matters*: real sympathy, based on feeling of another's feeling. Then it is literally true that whenever we add to another's suffering or joy,

God feels it.

Would it help to convey that belief to parents who are tempted to abuse their children or people tempted to torture animals? As long as people believe that we have to have a big adult human brain in order to feel much, they may rationalize all manner of cruelty. What about ongoing human practices such as separating the newborn from their mothers (try that with a mother bear sometime!) and circumcising the males—and females, around the world?

Most people can't care for a God who doesn't care for us, who is some sort of disembodied mind, without any feeling for us. We may already know some people too much like that already. So the idea of a God who actually feels and cares for us is what is so appealing about the theology of people like Rabbi Harold Kushner, whose theology echoes that of the Unitarian, Henry Nelson Wieman—another creative process theologian, who taught at the University of Chicago with Charles Hartshorne. Those holding this religious view have rejected the idea of a tyrant god in favor of a God of love. The third century Universalist, Origen, in Alexandria, Egypt, was an early proponent of this point of view. Another, more recent exception was Jules Lequier, whom I quoted at the beginning of this chapter.

If God cares for us, it is not as special creations who somehow deserve to transcend the limitations of individuality, but by means of sympathetic feeling and the ongoing memory of a mind that knows all (except the future in all its details), never forgets, and is made richer and deeper by our individual contributions.

We're not out of the woods yet. Let us say that God is actually affected and even changed by what we, the cells in God's body, feel, and do: that God's good health depends to some extent on ours because God feels everything and remembers it all. Then we must say that God feels the suffering caused by natural "acts of God," and feels both the sufferings of the tormented and also the sadistic pleasures of the tormentors. It may seem, then, that God feels all, equally, and doesn't take sides. Where's the morality in that?

To make ethical sense, we shall need to believe that, while God feels even the satisfactions of tormentors, God is actually tormented by them. If so, then God is not a mere receptacle for our feelings but responds to them from an innate sense of goodness and love. God's nature then includes the most far-reaching ethical sensitivity, which means that God remains to some degree in torment until all suffering is ended. That is not a happy thought.

How could it ever come about, that all suffering ends? Not easily, or quickly, for certain. But, if you believe in a God of love, then that is what God is trying to lead us to: change in the direction of less suffering and more loving. That—and only that—is doing God's work. And those who work in another way, or who are indifferent, are opposing God's work.

You may object: "And what in the world is God doing? Surely it is not in God's nature to suffer passively! Surely God would act against evil!" But what would you have God do? Should God have arranged that one of Hitler's epileptic seizures be terminal? And if God's powers do not extend to such matters, what can God do? Two thousand years ago, Jesus said that the sun shines and the rain falls on good and bad alike. But he also held the belief that God would soon intervene, unmistakably. It didn't happen, and his belief is not shared by educated people in our time. So it appears that God's work is left to us.

You might say: "But that's the way it's always been—and look what a mess we've made of things! It's too big a burden. We need special help." Isn't that to say we want to be treated as children? We exempt children from responsibility because they need to grow up first. Are we so immature that this is the treatment we require? A cartoon character says, "Sometimes I'd like to ask God why He created the Universe with so much poverty, hunger, and misery when He could have done something about it." Another character asks, "Well, why don't you?" The first one answers, "Because I'm afraid God might ask me the same question."

Whatever we might think or wish, it appears that God has decided to treat us as adults, leaving us responsible for what we do or fail to do. Then, you might say, a world in which God leaves us free to do evil and be treated like adults looks very much like a world with no God at all. But appearances may deceive us.

Let's think again about ourselves and our cells. Just as it is not in our power to arrange specifically for one of our cells to undertake a specific mission, so apparently, it is not in God's power to *suspend* the laws of cause and effect and chance and the purposes of individuals in order to arrange for a Hitler to have a fatal epileptic seizure or for hurricanes to be supernaturally diverted. However, this is not to say that we have absolutely no effect on our cells or that God has no influence on us.

This influence is not that of a tyrant, but of a loving God, whose method is to try to persuade us to do what is in our best interests, as well as the best interests of all concerned—in other words, of appealing to our better natures. This appeal, this persuasion is enacted whenever we come to realize the benefits of cooperation over competition, of negotiation over violence, of sharing over greed, and of respect for the natural environment.

If God is at work, luring us toward what is good, then our resistance or inattention adds to divine suffering, and it is not the case that time heals because God does not forget. The only way in which time can heal is by our overcoming evil in the world. What this boils down to is a conviction that requires more ethical behavior, more good social action, than any of the ways of believing that focus on individual salvation.

In June 1997, the Rev. Jozsef Szombatfalvi addressed the General Assembly of the Unitarian Universalist Association. He was the head of the Unitarian Minister's Association of Transylvania—one of the two countries (the other being Poland) where Unitarianism began over 400 years ago. He spoke about ". . . the burden of the legacy of 40 years of Communism and totalitarianism on us, which tried to destroy our faith and our spirit. And its aftermath still overshadows our life." He spoke of the Unitarians in Hungary and Romania and their faith in God as "the only sustaining power" that allowed them to "go against adversity and keep our spiritual-cultural-religious integrity. Affirming our Unitarian rational faith, we try to bring some meaning into this unfair collective suffering," he said. And he reached a compelling conclusion: "I think the real barrier is mostly within us . . . We need to learn to forgive and trust each other. We must have ideals and believe in them and never betray them and each other again; we need to produce honest and committed leadership from among us . . . we want to translate our beliefs into action. We want to be co-workers with God in creating our new heaven and earth, adding our will and sacrifice and love to it." Finally, speaking to American Unitarian Universalists who had given their support, he said how important it is for the Unitarians in Transylvania ". . . to know that somebody is behind us, encouraging, loving us, sharing wisdom and resources, caring for us, morally supporting us. It is important that we are not alone with our pain and joy, our failures and successes . . . God has sent you to us so that we together can create new heavens and a new earth. And for this we give thanks to the Creator and to you, the co-creators."

I trust there are many who may be moved by such an appeal, who may be persuaded by this idea, of being a co-creator. We are co-creators whenever we heed the appeal of love, whenever we give something of ourselves to lessen the suffering and further the happiness in the world.

Does it make God happy when we give of ourselves in order to lighten the load of others? Or is the ultimate Being unmoved by our joys and sufferings? A responsive and responsible God *must* be affected and even changed by what we feel, think, and do.

When we ponder cases of suicide bombers and other crazed killers of innocent people, we may ask, "Isn't evil what happens when some minds lose their connection with the human family?" And "Isn't this isolation a form of insanity?"

If you can experience the world in which you live as full of feeling, then you know yourself to be related to other living beings in such a way that your own joy and suffering cannot be known apart from theirs. Once you reach that point, there's no turning back. The old commander God who insists on our good behavior, whether we like it or not, becomes irrelevant to the issue of evil. Instead, it is up to all of us to realize that we are free and responsible to treat others respectfully. If that doesn't come naturally, we are out of contact. We need to re-connect.

[1] Charles Hartshorne, *Omnipotence and Other Theological Mistakes*. Albany: State University of New York Press, 1984, p. 18.
[2] Charles Hartshorne, p. 28.

Chapter Seven

Our Future As Individuals

Our consciousness may survive death.

"The wolf and the hawk, the crow and the salmon are brothers. The least and the greatest are one. You are the child of the forest and the sky. And the father of forever." ~*Native American*

The answer to the question of whether there is a God, or whether God is worthy of our worship, should not depend on whether we survive death with our consciousness intact. Gratitude is the appropriate response to the creativity of the universe, regardless of whether that creativity grants us some sort of thoughtful existence beyond physical death. Thankfulness for the gift of life—with no conditions attached—is the primary religious response.

Still, we may want to know whether we survive death in any sense. Or do our lives end in death? How could that ever be the case, if "end in" death means "becomes nothing but" dead? As Charles Hartshorne pointed out, that idea is absurd. "A conscious state of life cannot *become* an unconscious state of being dead . . . When we write the biography of a person we are not describing a corpse or heap of dust. We are describing a stream of experiences .

. . ." of which a corpse is not capable.[1] We are describing the *reality* of past events.

What is the past? "What is history about if yesterday's or last year's or last century's events are now simply unreal? . . . apart from our knowledge of the past we know virtually nothing." This is because what exists now is what we have not yet had time to know, and the future is yet to be determined. Conscious knowledge is knowledge of the past. As C.S. Peirce put it, "The past is the sum of accomplished facts." And, "It is the past which is actual." This is taking time seriously. Whitehead summed up this way of looking at time and reality by saying that, once an event has occurred, it is a permanent item in reality. It is an accomplished fact that cannot be de-accomplished or nullified.

The permanence of the past is made evident to us as we consult our memory, but our capacity for memory is limited. We may become distressed by that realization as we grow older. If, however, God is the body and mind of the Universe, then God does not lose what God has acquired. Our conscious lives remain forever as actual accomplishments and as our contributions to God's ever-conscious life.

Our lives have been likened to books and works of art that have beginnings and endings. They are all finite entities. Only so, is it possible for them to have definite form and distinctiveness. To be an individual, unless you are God, is to be limited in time and space—to be mortal. Death may end our conscious lives, but death cannot be the destruction of everything we have achieved. What we have accomplished is our gift to the world and to the divine life. It is our objective immortality.

Is that enough? Some will say, "No. If I do not remain a conscious self after I die, then I will cease to exist, having no awareness of anything, including my contribution to the divine life—so it won't matter to me." True enough, but consider: if you had the capacity to be everlasting in time, then why shouldn't you also have the capacity to be everlasting in space—in short, to be a god? Some say that is just the sort of thing we have in store for us: to become angels. I know of no way of confirming or denying that expectation, short of dying and (perhaps) seeing what happens.

It would seem that God alone is capable of an eternal individuality: unborn and undying, experiencing the entire past and future through the creative process. Then we are to God as cells to a superorganism. The belief that God created us uniquely set aside from the rest of creation as deserving of special treatment would make of God a mere means to our everlasting happiness. Better that we go with the wisdom of a Jewish ritual that says that God "gives to our fleeting days abiding significance." If we are grateful for the gift of life, we should not need to insist that we are shortchanged unless we survive it.

Who will appreciate your experience when you are no longer alive? Those who remember you will gradually die out. As Hartshorne said, "The adequate appreciation of your life can only be in a Life that transcends all other life in its undying power to participate in the satisfactions of others. The adequate recipient of the contributions of each moment of experience can only be divine."[2]

Whether we believe in the continuation of our individual spiritual lives after physical death or not, we may choose to be grateful for the fact that each of us has been blessed with the opportunity to create something uniquely our own to give back as an offering to the eternal life of the divine creative process, of whose life we are blessed to be a part. For what more should we ask? ". . . our existence from moment to moment 'enriches the divine life.' And that is the meaning of our existence."[3]

Is that truly all there is to the meaning of our existence? What are we to make of a widespread indigenous view that immortality is found in the ongoing community that extends indefinitely? Upholding that view, Malidoma Patrice Somé asserted that physical death does not end our lives but results in a different manner of our belonging to the community. Life is defined by growth, decline and regeneration. "Having journeyed adequately in this world in your life, you become much more effective to the community that contained you when you return to the world of Spirit. When my grandfather died, he told my father, 'I have to go now. From where I'll be, I'll be more useful to you than if I have to stay here.' Death is not a separation but a different form of communion, a higher form of connectedness with the community, providing an opportunity for even greater service."[4] According to this view, such service is rendered by means of what, in our culture, is called "paranormal" communication between those who walk on the earth and those who continue on to live in the world both beyond and within the one we ordinarily perceive.

There is a widespread belief that the divine is infused in our world in such a manner that our own primary nature is not material, but spiritual, and that, in order to exist as material beings, we have had to "contract." As Somé explains it, "To fit ourselves into the narrow part of the universe that allows energy to exist as matter takes some getting used to, and we only bother with it at all because it serves the useful and unavoidable purpose of expanding the spirit in us. It is as if in order to expand or to grow, one must contract or squeeze. The contracted form of our volatile spirit is the body. The adventures of the body prepare the spirit for the leap into its next phase of growth."[5] How far removed that conviction is from the common view in our country, that growth stops with death, and that any afterlife must be one of eternal reward or punishment!

Some's assertion is based on the Native experience of communication with the dead, which is taken for granted even by many people of our culture. What, indeed, are we to make of the many testimonials to "life after life" that have been published? Are those of us who haven't had such experiences wise to discount them? Some scientists seem adept at explaining away such experiences. Dreading as I do the prospect of a permanent loss of consciousness, I'd prefer to believe in (a pleasant sort of) life after life. It seems to me foolish to rule that out. But, with the modern discoveries concerning how our brains work (or don't, in cases of disorders), it appears that the burden of evidence is on those of us who hold out for consciousness as something more than what the brain does.

As I have indicated, I believe there is such evidence and that consciousness needs to be understood in a more expansive sense than is usually the case. Long-term and extensive research at Princeton and Stanford Universities and ample anecdotal reporting with which I am familiar suggests that ordinary people have some capacity for seeing into the future as well as into a time before their own birth.[6] Research with practicing "mediums" has shown that they are typically able to produce more than 80 pieces of information about deceased relatives. In one extensive study, researchers achieved an accuracy rate of 83%, one of them being right 93% of the time. A control group of non-mediums were right 36% of the time.

It seems reasonable to me that The Field of life-energy, in addition to generating, maintaining and healing us, may also carry our consciousness beyond the grave. That would be an energetic explanation for reincarnation—which is still believed in by many people all over the world: The Field animates a body that grows to fullness by its power. It maintains that body for a while; and then, at death, that portion of it returns to the cosmic energy stream. I see no reason why The Field cannot carry consciousness, and the emotion behind consciousness, beyond the physicality of the human body. I differ with Hartshorne, as he made up his mind about this issue fairly early in life, and never wavered. For me, it's still an open question.

As I have pondered the issue of time, I have balked at the common notion of beyond-death existence being timeless. If time is an essential aspect of reality, then an existing spiritual world would also exist in time. Also, I have become more open to the possibility of a real spiritual world, having spoken with many people who have told me of their experiences. Recently, I met with an American Indian seer friend who told me some specifics concerning my first wife Joyce who had died. She had remained a good friend, and after she had departed, my seer friend told me some things about Joyce that amounted to more than good guessing. There is no way she could have known about some of those "communications" on her own.

Even so, I still like the attitude expressed by Henry David Thoreau, who, as he lay dying and was asked what he expected, answered: "One world at a time."

[1] Charles Hartshorne, *Omnipotence and Other Theological Mistakes*. Albany: State University of New York, 1984, p. 32f.
[2] Charles Hartshorne, "Taking Freedom Seriously," Lowell lecture, presented by the Cambridge Forum, Nov., 1983.
[3] Charles Hartshorne, *Omnipotence and Other Theological Mistakes*, p. 27.
[4] Malidoma Patrice Somé, *The Healing Wisdom of Africa*. NY: Tarcher/Putnam, 1998, p. 53.
[5] Somé, p. 61.
[6] Lynne McTaggart, *The Field*, p. 195.

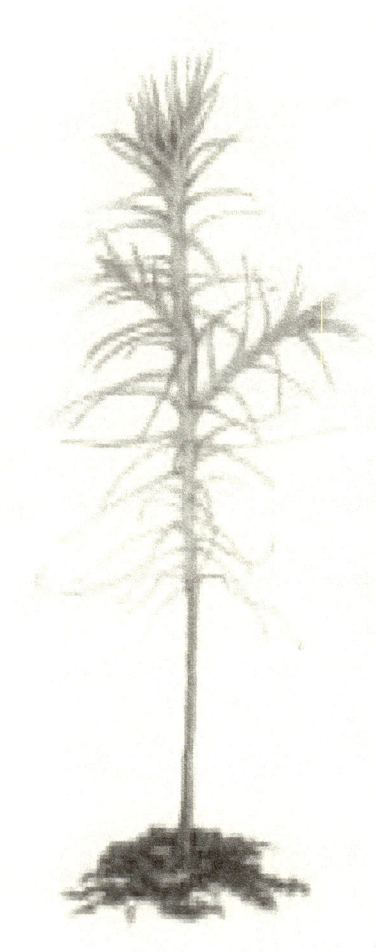

PART V

MENDING THE SEVERED CENTER

"Let me be inwardly attuned to thy harmony, Great Universe." ~*Marcus Aurelius*

"A human being is part of the whole, called by us the 'Universe,' a part limited in time and space. He experiences himself, his thoughts and feelings, as something separate from the rest—a kind of optical delusion of his consciousness. This delusion is a kind of prison for us, restricting us to our personal desires and to affection to a few persons nearest to us. Our task must be to free ourselves from this prison by widening our circle of compassion to embrace all living creatures and the whole of nature in its beauty." ~*Albert Einstein, reported in* **The New York Post***, November 28, 1972*

In parts one and two we examined examples of loss of connection in human life and thought, especially in the religions. Parts three and four were focused on the foundations of connection in human nature and in the natural world as a whole. This last part is devoted to ways in which humanity may reconnect, through our morality, our relationship to the natural world, our ways of healing, and our practice of worship.

Chapter One

The Foundation of Morality

We live in a universe of value. Morality is based, not on following rules, but on one's sense of connection.

"How should we relate to beings who look into mirrors and see themselves as individuals, who mourn companions and may die of grief, who have a consciousness of 'self'? Don't they deserve to be treated with the same sort of consideration we accord to other highly sensitive beings— ourselves?" *~Jane Goodall*

"Our morality should teach us that our long-run goal must transcend mere personal advantage." *~Charles Hartshorne*

The biologist, Jacques Monod, summed up our ethical predicament: "No society before ours was ever rent by contradictions so agonizing. Both primitive and classical cultures saw knowledge and values stemming from the same source. For the first time in history a civilization is trying to shape itself while clinging desperately to the tradition to justify its values and at the same time abandoning it as the source of knowledge."[1] The tradition Monod referred to is the religious tradition of Western civilization, based on Judeo-Christian values, as influenced by Greek philosophy and Zoroastrianism. As usually interpreted, these values boil down to a system of rewards and punishments.

When people have a belief in rewards and punishments, such as in heaven and hell, it makes sense to hold to self-interest as the final court of appeal: do as you're told, or you are punished; believe the right thing, and you are rewarded. It comes down to self-interest. This is why hedonism (pleasure or happiness is the sole or chief good in life) and egoism (individual self-interest is the actual motive of all conscious action) are the predominant ethical philosophies of the West.

Combine self-interest as the ultimate ethical principle with a belief in rewards and punishments for one's behavior, and you get some such doctrine as the old heaven and hell arrangement, which the Russian philosopher, Berdyaev, aptly called "the most disgusting morality ever conceived."

Charles Hartshorne put it this way: "If to be good is to be loving, how can we motivate good behavior by rewards and threats? What have they to do with love of neighbors? If we love people, we want to help them. How can doing what we want to do require a reward, beyond the satisfaction of having a rational aim and the capacity to realize it? Unless loving is its own reward it is not really loving."[2]

The theme of this book is loss of connection and the possibility of re-connection with the entire natural world. Our story of the universe and the human role in the universe is our primary source of intelligibility. It must also become our primary source of value. The philosopher, C.S. Peirce said as much when he attributed to the ultimate good " . . . the same kind of being that a law of nature has, making it lie in the rationalization of the universe" *(Collected Papers of Charles Sanders Peirce, Vol. I,* Cambridge: Harvard University Press, 1960, 1.590).

This idea, of value as an expression of the evolution of the universe, is at the heart of a natural ethics. That is why I have focused on the sense of estrangement that our Western Judeo-Christian story—and the "objective" view of Greek philosophy and modern science—have engendered and supported, and why I have paid such attention to cosmology, emotion, feeling and mind—in short, "the whole picture." Since we can no longer accept either the doctrines of religions presuming to be revealed or the philosophical doctrine of the fixed nature of things, we need to discover the foundation for our values within our experience of the universe as it is.

Some philosophers insist that any claim that we discover values by looking into matters of fact involves us in a "naturalistic fallacy"—trying to derive values from fact, when values can never be so derived, because values are not facts; they are of a different logical category. I believe they are wrong. I have never been able to see how values can be derived from anything but fact. Disagreements about values invariably boil down to disagreements about fact: which facts are true, relevant, important to someone, and so on. How else but by pointing to some fact could we ever explain why we believe something is right or good? To the persistent question, "But what makes it 'good'?" we can only respond either that it's good because some presumed authority says so, or that it's good because it increases our well-being and sense of connection with others—and even that it's good because it increases the well-being of the whole earth community—that being the largest possible ethical ideal. The first approach has caused us a lot of trouble; there's reason for hope in the second as long as we pay due homage to the connection-with-others part.

A primary problem with values in our culture is that people have tried to derive them as a solely human concern, from the belief that we are the only creatures for whom morality matters. On that basis, people have presumed the corollary, that non-human lives, not being concerned with morality, don't matter as we do. In the language of current economic theories concerning the environment, they are all "external," and, therefore, have no recognizable value. We can hardly underestimate the enormous damage humans have done to the whole earth community as a result of this flawed thinking.

Our need to derive our values from the universe, rather than a presumed privileged position, is urgent: we are in the process of making the earth uninhabitable for all but a small percentage of the species that lived prior to our industrial revolution. No doubt the reader has seen many litanies to that effect. I shall not belabor the point.

The self-emergent and self-governing processes of the universe are also its value manifestations. We must come to see how this is so. Thomas Berry and Brian Swimme have noted how the universe embodies the values of differentiation, subjectivity and communion. If we were to take these three values seriously, we should be able to see, for example, how the democratic process in the self-government of societies is more nature-connected than any autocratic system. This is because the democratic process is founded on respect for individuals who have minds of their own and who are also in a cooperative relationship with one another.

The foundation of morality is not to be found in any system of thought that boils down to "Do as you're told." As we have seen, the God of the universe is not that sort of God, not a tyrant. The God of love works by means of freedom and an appeal to our better natures. There is nothing ethical about deciding whether to obey what some call God's commands. Deciding whether to obey someone, even God, isn't ethical; it's practical. It is based on nothing more than our belief concerning the consequences. Such a decision comes down to a matter of self-interest: *here's what's in it for me if I obey, or not.*

Re-connecting with the real world, ethical decision-making occurs when we are confronted with a choice between two goods (or evils): do I tell the truth, and thereby hurt someone? Do I fudge on my income tax in order better to provide for my family, or am I scrupulously honest for the sake of the larger community? *How Good People Make Tough Decisions* by Rushworth Kidder is an excellent treatment of this subject. As the author indicates, of the various ethical philosophies, the soundest boils down to "Don't treat someone else in a way in which you would not want to be treated." Asking "why not?" suggests a lack of connection, an inability to recognize that "the other" is like you. This is why we must have laws and the means of their enforcement. As long as people aren't well-connected, they cannot be trusted to treat each other respectfully.

The universal foundation of morality is the sense of connection. An African saying has it well stated: "I am as we are." How is it that someone will go well out of the way to perform an act of kindness, with no reward other than the satisfaction of having helped someone? It can only be an embedded conviction that "this other person and I are so much alike that when I hurt him/her, I hurt myself."

Why are we moved by the soulful eyes of caged primates? By loon calls or the howling of wolves? What about bats? How many of us feel any sense of likeness with them? And then, snakes? Spiders? How far does your sense of connection extend? That is the primary ethical question. How wide is your circle of empathy? The wideness of one's circle will depend, at least in part, on one's sense of communicability. In his book, *Mind of the Raven*, Bernd Heinrich writes of the expressiveness of ravens who, once a trusting relationship is established with a human being, are able to communicate, not only emotions, but intentions. They remember faces. They certainly have moods and are capable of sharing food and other resources.

Headline: "Scientists produce 'ratbox'—first radio-controlled animal." "Neuroscientists announced yesterday that they have created the world's first radio-controlled animal by wiring a computer chip directly into the brain of a living rat . . . The new 'ratbox,' funded in part by the U.S. military, can be equipped with a miniature video camera and might one day be used to find victims in buildings after an earthquake or bombing, according to the research team. But in imposing a primitive form of mind control, the researchers acknowledge that the technology takes science into challenging ethical territory." One of the researchers acknowledges:

"Personally, I think there is something creepy about the whole idea. But that's only because we are not used to it."[3]

Presumably, like so much else that's creepy in our culture, we'll get used to it. The creepy feeling will disappear. It would be better if we inquired into that creepy feeling. It may derive from some sense of connection with that helpless little animal. Losing the creepy feeling is losing the connection. Is that a good thing?

The only trustworthy basis for morality is a sense of connection. This is so because that sense is rooted in the universe itself. The question is, how wide does that sense range in our own lives? As far as loved ones? Friends? Non-threatening animals? What is the nature of our connection to perceived enemies? "Dangerous" animals? Pathogens? Other planets? Other galaxies? To what and for what reasons do we feel a sense of connection?

When we find ourselves engaged in a profound disagreement with someone—perhaps even a life-threatening situation—the only hope for reconciliation is to find some common ground, some way of connecting. "Getting to Yes," depends on it, as the Roger Fisher book by that title explains.

The ultimate foundation for human morality is universal. It upholds lessons taught by the story of the Universe. The primary lesson is the realization that all selves, all souls, are members of the self-expression of the Universe. We know the life of the Universe almost exclusively through our participation in the Earth's story. For all practical purposes, our morality must be an earth-centered morality. Former U.S. Senator and Vice President, Al Gore, echoed that view in his book, *Earth In the Balance*, when he wrote that concern for the environment must become "the central organizing principle of civilization."[4]

The Rev. Dr. David E. Bumbaugh, when Associate Professor of Ministry at Meadville/Lombard Theological School at the University of Chicago, highlighted the ethic that extends beyond the individual to the whole earth community when he wrote, "We are driven to recognize a paradox: our sense of separateness is ultimately an illusion, yet our individual separateness is a consequence of the drive of the universe for differentiation and complexity. We are driven by our story to seek an ethic that respects the individual *and* the ground out of which the individual emerges. This implies a deep concern for ecological justice that reaches across class, racial, ethnic, even species distinctions and embraces a vision that responds to the largest sense of self we are capable of entertaining."[6]

Such an enlarged ethical vision may yet enable us to turn from the destructive course engendered by the old *subdue and conquer* fantasy and become, instead, agents of healing and cooperation with earth's self-governance.

[1]Jacques Monod, *Chance and Necessity*. NY: Vintage Books, 1972, p. 171.
[2]Charles Hartshorne, *Omnipotence and Other Theological Mistakes*, p. 99.
[3]"Scientists produce 'ratbox,'" by Gareth Cook, *Boston Globe*, May 2, 2002.
[4]Al Gore, *Earth In the Balance*. Boston: Houghton Mifflin Co, 1992, p. 269.
[5]David E. Bumbaugh, "Everywhere Incarnate," article in *The World*, published by the Unitarian Universalist Association, Boston. Nov./Dec. 2001.

Chapter Two

Respecting Nature

On the importance of biodiversity and sustainability and a sense of intimacy with and responsibility for the earth community: A "green" religious revival.

"You can't argue with nature. It is the primary context for living and for everything alive." ~Bernd Heinrich

"We hurt because we see the land being destroyed. We believe in the wild earth because it's the religion we're born with." ~*Thomas Gilbert, Arctic Village chief and elder*

"Instead of ... trying to impose our will on Nature, we should be quiet and listen to what she has to tell us ... Life is a miracle beyond our comprehension, and we should reverence it even when we have to struggle against it ... Humbleness is in order; there is no excuse for scientific conceit." ~*Rachel Carson*

The universe is composed of about 100 billion galaxies, each of which contains hundreds of billions of stars, a great number of which probably feature solar systems. Some solar systems have been located. There is good reason to believe that many of them contain planets much like ours, which suggests that there are living creatures feeling and thinking in some manner throughout the universe. Being many light years away from us, intelligent contact with them seems an insurmountable problem. But who knows? Other insurmountable problems have been addressed with some success.

How arrogant, how presumptuous it would be to suppose that we humans are superior to all other life forms or that we are a special creation with a unique destiny apart from the rest of the universe. Our selves have no existence and no meaning apart from the immense web of selves that make up the universe.

The universe does not center on human beings any more than it does on any other of its centers, which, as we have come to realize, are everywhere. We are not the only creatures to experience pain and pleasure or to enter into sympathetic relations with others. "Subdue and dominate" is a perverse basis for understanding our ethical relationship to the world.

How is it that so many people in our culture have such trouble seeing that our survival—not to mention that of other species— depends upon our developing a lasting respect for the earth? How can so many be taken up in sadistic fantasies of a cataclysmic Armageddon resulting in eternal separation of the saved from the damned, so that, for them, the fate of the earth is of no consequence?

We humans have gotten ourselves into a lot of trouble by denying the natural world as the meeting place of the divine and human and, instead, holding up our own words (in the form of sacred books) as supreme in that regard. This denial has made possible the conception of the natural world as a mere collection of external objects. That objectifying attitude has proven catastrophic. Our insistence that the human is the only spiritual being with an eternal destiny quite other than that of the other members of the created world has resulted in the severing of our ties with the larger earth community.

But now we may take heart from the fact that many thoughtful people, in religion as well as in science, are able to see, and these fellow humans say that the path we need to take must involve our coming to view ourselves as participants in a complex and fragile web of relationships in which each creature is valuable. A bright human future may be achieved as we learn how to live more in intimacy with the earth community.

Recognizing our deep kinship with other life forms is the key to our survival and fulfillment. We have denied their role in our lives for too long. We must learn how to hear their pain and see how they suffer when we harm them. The primatologist Frans de Waal coined the term "anthropodenial" to describe blindness to the humanlike characteristics of other species. While it remains true that life feeds on life and that we must kill to live, that is no excuse for causing unnecessary suffering of individual animals, much less the wanton destruction of whole habitats.

Much of humanity is still largely in a tragic state of denial concerning the extensive damage that we are doing to the earth's web of life. This denial is especially strong in the United States of America, one of the most polluting countries in the world *and* the country that has the greatest resources for addressing this issue. Too many of us seem unable to move from a self-centered conviction that we are earth's glory to a realization that we are the most destructive and dangerous animal ever to move on earth's surface and through its oceans and atmosphere.

Refusal to accept limitations on human growth has resulted in pollution and disruption of ecological communities throughout the planet and in the extinction of numerous species. This extinction proceeds at an unprecedented rate. As Thomas Berry has noted, ". . . there exists in our tradition a hidden rage against those inner as well as outer forces that create limits on our activities. Some ancient force in the Western psyche seems to perceive limitation as a demonic obstacle to be eliminated, rather than as a strengthening discipline. Acceptance of the challenging aspect of the natural world is a primary condition for creative intimacy with the natural world."[1]

As the climate changes at an alarming rate and the earth and oceans heat up, threatening our very existence, we are faced with a fundamental question: can we learn that it is necessary to make some sacrifices for the well-being of the earth-community as a whole? Failure even to consider this question lies at the root of the American dilemma. Life includes hardships of many kinds. To avoid all hardship that can possibly be evaded is to choose a lesser life. One telling example of the insistence that life be experienced free of disturbing feelings is the widespread avoidance of anxiety through the use of feeling-deadening drugs that do not cure, as some forms of therapy can. Americans spend a great deal of our time and energy trying to get and keep comfortable to the point where we often miss the actual enjoyments afforded when we are willing to risk some discomfort.

How can we not cry out as we learn that we have turned the ocean into a garbage dump where whales and turtles swallow many pounds of plastic. And soon there will be more plastic than fish!

The impact of human population growth and wasteful consumption on the biological diversity of the planet is proving to be disastrous. As Edward Abbey put it, "Growth for the sake of growth is the ideology of the cancer cell." Human prosperity, even in the information age, still rests on the foundation of a diverse natural world. The more species an ecosystem has, the more stable and productive it will be.

Vandana Shiva pointed out the importance of biodiversity: "Biodiversity is the key to sustainability. It is the basis of mutuality and reciprocity—the 'law of return' based on the recognition of the right of all species to happiness and freedom from suffering. Yet the law of return based on freedom and diversity is being replaced by the logic of return on investments. Genetic engineering, even while preying on the world's biological diversity, threatens to aggravate the ecological crisis through the expansion of monocultures and monopolies."

After declaring that "An intolerance of diversity is the biggest threat to peace in our times," Shiva explained that "The cultivation of diversity involves reclaiming the right to self-organize for those coerced into living by imposed measures. For the dominant groups of nations and humans who impose their priorities and patterns on the living diversity of peoples and other species, the cultivation of diversity involves seeing the capacity and intrinsic value of the 'other'—other cultures and other species. It involves giving up the will to control, an imperative rooted in the fear of that which is free, a fear that gives rise to violence. The cultivation of diversity is, therefore, a nonviolent response to the violence of globalization, homogenization, and monocultures."[2]

Some suggest that accepting the responsibility of environmental stewardship need not require Draconian government regulation, but that, instead, we should be able to rely on non-governmental organizations, private corporations and intelligent use of the free market. I could be more convinced of that perspective if I weren't writing at a time of almost daily revelations of corporate greed and even illegalities that include participation by prominent people in the government. Even the most honest applications of the current economic system would fail to address the issue of environmental degradation because we are still saddled with the disastrous assumption that environmental concerns are "externals" in economic terms, which is to say that we need not factor them into our economic accounting. There are a few attempts now in practice to make these "externals" count, but we have a long way to go before this issue is properly addressed.

We must not evade the crucial role of government in seeing to it that economic concerns—making money, plain and simple—don't override the common interests of the whole earth community. Government regulations and their enforcement are essential to earth-respecting economics. Yet, I write this as we experience the most disastrous governmental energy and environmental policy and practice in the history of our country. Our government refuses to fund contraception, claiming abortion as the reason, yet abortion rates lessen when prevention is readily accessible. Our government continues to subsidize fossil fuel industries and allow them to write our nation's energy policy. At a time when safe, clean and renewable energy sources like wind and solar power are the fastest growing and most affordable energy sources, government officials continue to favor the polluters funding their political campaigns.

Whenever someone calls for government support for clean energy, we hear the complaint: "That's socialism! Let the free market work!" Yet these same people would have us taxpayers pay many billions of dollars to subsidize the oil, gas, coal, nuclear, and utility industries. Our voices will have to be loud, clear and persistent to be heard by the officials in the executive branch who have much of their personal investments sunk in the "old guard" energy sector. If Americans had put their tax dollars into clean energy alternatives instead of lining the pockets of the polluters, our country and the world would be a much cleaner and safer place in which to live.

Our nation continues to reject the global framework for addressing climate change, claiming that our economy will suffer if we do so. Why haven't the other nations—who also have economies to protect—taken the same position? Because, unlike ours, their leaders are able to see what must be done if humanity is to reverse a terribly irresponsible course.

Greed is the problem. When money enters the picture, people often substitute it for love. And too many Americans act out of greed and complacency as a result. They still seem to believe that we were born with an inalienable right to waste as much as we think we need to and use far more than our share of the world's resources, just so long as we remain comfortable.

We would not be assaulting the earth as we are if we were able to see and hear what is right before us: an earth-community of "subjects," creatures, all of whom share something of the same feelings and mentality that animates us. Our industrial eyes and ears are closed to their sufferings as we bulldoze the tops off mountains, poison the atmosphere and cover the oceans and animals with oil slicks and plastic waste.

A natural sense of what economics is really all about has emerged from some ecologists and even a few economists, like Herman E. Daly, Edward Goldsmith and David Korten. From their writings, we learn that the threat to both economics and religion is from a single source: the disruption of the natural world. Writers such as Thomas Berry point out that economics and religion are two aspects of a single earth process, and that, therefore, we need to experience a sense of the sacred character of the natural world as the primary revelation of the divine. We must learn to see ourselves as part of a process whereby the universe reflects on and celebrates itself if we are to have enough spiritual staying-power to see ourselves through the trying times ahead.

An important example of the corporate takeover of common natural resources involves the "free trade" of water, which is in direct conflict with the sustainable ideal of access by the poor to land, water resources and other agricultural inputs. Companies like Bechtel, Enron and Monsanto, along with French companies, are busy buying water utilities and then raising prices on their "products." The result in some areas is immense suffering as water reserves are disappearing due to overuse. Two-thirds of our human communities depend directly on land, water, and biodiversity for their livelihoods. The destruction—or privatization—of land, water, and biodiversity creates poverty for the people who are left without food, water and means of livelihood; however, in the commercial economy, this destruction registers as "growth" or even "progress."

In Arizona, Hopi and Navaho Indians are distressed about sacred springs, streams and wells that are drying up because an energy company removes over a billion gallons of water each year from the aquifer underlying the land in order to move crushed coal in underground slurry lines to a Nevada power plant that fuels the bright lights of Las Vegas, Phoenix, and Los Angeles. During the 1990s, Native Americans made some progress in securing protection for many sacred places; however, a number of decisions by the government have overturned those gains. Again, Native American concerns for the eco-system are deemed secondary to the profits of the resource-extraction industries.

It is essential to understand that the issue before us is not what the commercial interests insist it is: a choice between environment or development, ecology or poverty. It is between resource-destructive economies based on privatization of resources versus resource-conserving economies based on sharing of the earth's gifts of land, water and biodiversity. The challenge is this: will the earth's resources sustain the livelihoods of all the people, or will they generate profits for the huge corporations? This is not a narrowly political issue; it is a whole earth issue. It is time to bring economy back to its roots in ecology. Peace, justice and sustainability require no less.

There are still reasons for hope as more and more people are waking up to the real crisis we now face. Some creative experiments are taking place throughout the world that aim to accord economic value to forests, wetlands, even insects, in short, all of nature's gifts—renewable as long as we don't exploit them to the point of destruction. Using such accounting methods, Costa Rica reduced its rate of deforestation from one of the world's highest to one of the lowest. Another sign of hope: in 2002, Guatemalan loggers agreed to a U.S. Agency for International Development project that helps protect the rainforest by giving local communities a stake in its survival. Illegal logging and forest fires had consumed two-thirds of Guatemala's rain forests, and it was expected that, if something were not done to curb logging, the forest would be gone in a short time. The long-term result remains to be seen, but giving local people a say in their own survival is surely a positive development.

However, as I write, the rainforest of Brazil is being destroyed in favor of farming, despite the essential role of rainforests in capturing carbon. This is happening as there is an international outcry. The response so far from their president is to the effect that "The Amazon belongs to us, so **we** make the decisions about it." This flies in the face of knowing that rainforests and trees around the world are the earth's lungs. The Peterson Institute for International Economics has just issued a report saying that, at the current rate of deforestation, the Amazonian rainforest could reach an irreversible tipping point as early as 2021.

Getting our own national government back on the right track should be our urgent concern. That will require being politically active, like it or not.

Cities, including New York City and Boston, have initiated plans to keep their water pure by restoring the health of the rivers and forests that are the sources of that water, which is less costly than building new filtration plants. "Conservation banking" is a recent and growing practice; however, even the best conservation banks cannot replace the range of services provided by the pieces of nature sacrificed for development. But at least they are establishing a value for work done by nature.

Although there probably are other such planets, we know of no other world with such stunning self-expression as the earth. What keeps us from experiencing this beautiful blue planet as an ongoing celebration of life? As Thomas Berry and Brian Swimme have emphasized, unless we are able to become "entranced" as members of the earth community, it is unlikely that we will have the psychic energy required for the earth's renewal. That entrancement can only be the result of our sense of communion with the natural world, and that can only come from our capacity to appreciate and empathize with the thoughts and feelings of other natural beings through our direct contact with nature.

Many humans are now experiencing a religious revival: not like the obnoxious examples usually presented on television, but rather a growing realization that the primary sacred community is the universe itself, with the whole earth community being the obvious immediate subject of concern. This is a heartening development.

Members of the Green political movements have seen how both capitalism and socialism have viewed human labor and natural resources as commodities that reduce people and nature to exploitable, disposable resources.

They envision a democratic society that provides for its members in an ecologically sustainable manner. We may work within such a movement, or within one of the larger established parties, or simply work with others in our own community. Despite federal inaction on climate change, many American cities and states have programs to cut greenhouse gas emissions. States and cities have often led the way concerning change for the better as was true regarding the development of disability insurance, child labor and anti-monopoly laws. Some local communities, here and abroad, are leading the way in harmonizing people and the planet. Personal commitment is required, in any case.

The greatest scientists—Darwin being a splendid example— were not simply curious about nature. They loved nature. Darwin loved animals as his fellow creatures. He was able to spend a great deal of his time in the study of earthworms because he did not look down on them. The consequences of such an extended love can be enormous—and deeply needed in a world in which, too often, humanity has pitted itself against nature.

Nature writers like Loren Eiseley and Rachel Carson and naturalists like Jane Goodall and Sally Carrighar have helped us establish an acquaintance and even an affectionate relationship with individuals of other species within their own wilderness context. More contact with and respect for Native peoples can also be an exhilarating experience, beyond the educational value it affords.

Today we have animal liberation movements and many sorts of conservation movements whose objectives are to save nature from annihilation. But, like the related economic and political movements, they all need a philosophy to deepen the extent of their concerns. I trust that the creative process philosophy upheld in this book is just such a philosophy and that it offers a reasonable and accurate understanding of the connection between the human and the divine in nature.

[1] Thomas Berry, *The Great Work*. New York: Bell Tower, 1999, p. 67.
[2] Vandana Shiva, *Biopiracy: The Plunder of Nature and Knowledge*. Boston: South End Press, 1997, p. 87 and p. 199f.

Chapter Three

Natural Healing

Preventing armoring and achieving de-armoring
Re-connecting, by telling the story of the universe
Struggling against biopiracy
Protecting the ethnosphere

"There is something infinitely healing in the repeated refrains of nature." ~*Rachel Carson*

"We will not attain sustainability until we learn to love both nature and people. To love nature, you have to find a way to make a deep connection with it." ~*Daniel B. Botkin, biologist, Center for Study of the Environment at the University of California at Santa Barbara*

Natural healing involves us both as individuals and in relation to all other selves with whom we have conscious connections. For the individual, it is a matter of de-armoring. Regarding relationships with other humans and with non-human life, it means re-connecting.

No one knows when or why humankind first armored itself. By "armor," I am following Wilhelm Reich in referring to the pervasive chronic muscular contractions—knotted-ness—that prevent the free flow of energy through the human body. This somatic armoring is closely related to the character armor of the various personality types. People unfamiliar with this concept would do well to read Reich's *Character Analysis*. Regarding the origins of armoring, I think it is enough to say that early peoples often had a very hard life, and armoring was a way of protecting themselves, much as it is for infants, children, and adolescents today.

An important point to note is that armoring can include the brain as well as the rest of the body. It affects the way we perceive what we see, and it affects our thinking. It is not possible for brain-armored people to see or think clearly or in a healthy manner.

Ocular armor occurs early in life when infants are subjected to the hard or hateful looks of frustrated parents or medical personnel. Actual brain damage may result, in the form of armoring (blocked energy) at the base of the brain. That can cause schizophrenia. The standard treatment for schizophrenia is the prescription of anti-psychotic medication and supportive therapy, it being the common assumption that there is no cure, other than, perhaps, time. That common viewpoint reflects a lack of understanding of how energy blockages cause disease and, therefore, reveals ignorance concerning the curative process. When we read about the ongoing search for the defective gene or gene sequences that "cause" such diseases or disorders as schizophrenia and "bi-polar" disorder, not to mention the various cancers, we see no reference to energy flow or its blockage. While some disorders are clearly caused by defective genetic endowment (PKU, for example) and others by infection (AIDS), there are many diseases or disorders that, regardless of genetic endowment, are amenable to therapy, as long as the energetic basis of the condition is understood. Patients with full-blown cases of schizophrenia have been cured by Orgone therapy. One would think that would be of interest to anyone concerned with finding a cure for that dreaded disorder.

The first solution to the problem of armoring is prevention: gentle and contactful treatment of infants and children, especially when they are feeling frightened, angry, or sad. Children should always be allowed to express their feelings, including of course their sexual feelings, so long as they are not allowed to hurt others. An obvious indication of armoring is breath-holding or shallow breathing. When children are ordered to "stop crying," they must hold their breathing to stop the emotional expression. When breath is held, armoring occurs. If such situations are repeated, the armoring will become chronic and affect the character structure of the individual.

In cases of chronic armoring, individual therapy can work wonders, if it is done responsibly. I believe that the medical Orgonomists trained by Reich and those he put in charge of training are the most qualified, but there are other psychotherapists who are contactful enough to help people achieve increased healthy functioning. Regarding drug treatment: "Depression study finds therapy as effective as drugs" (*Boston Globe*, May 24, 2002). The article ends by acknowledging reports that ". . . suggest that placebos not only work as quickly as drugs in the short term, but affect the same areas of the brain." Psychoactive drug therapies are all founded on knowledge of the ways in which chemicals affect our emotional lives. What is much less well-known are the profound ways in which our emotional states can change our brain processing and cell chemistry. The key to understanding this issue is the manner in which energy is blocked or allowed to flow freely through the organism. In addition, there are any number of therapeutic experiences that may be helpful in the de-armoring and armor-prevention process. I refer to experiences as simple as swimming or walking, writing in a journal or telling your story to a sympathetic listener. There are body movement forms, such as Tai Chi, Yoga or Chi Gong that focus on paying careful attention to what is going on within oneself: breathing, eye contact, eye movement, awareness of tense areas, and so on—such forms may be helpful in letting go of armor that is not solidified.

I believe that the best bit of advice is to "follow the child" or, as in the gospel, "become as a child." Careful observation of the ways in which reasonably healthy infants and young children organize and express themselves tells us more about healthy functioning than any course or textbook. The Feldenkrais method of learning how our nervous system organizes our movements is a good example. I am told that Feldenkrais learned his method by observing infants and young children.

De-armoring is a way of natural healing but should not be viewed in isolation from its context, which is more and more being seen in terms of our existence within an inexhaustible sea of life-energy. All living things radiate this energy, and the characteristics of this emission indicate a lot about the healthy or unhealthy state of an organism. As he conducted extensive experiments on electromagnetic frequencies in living things, Dr. Robert O. Becker was able to stimulate or speed up regeneration of various sorts of tissues in humans and animals. He saw the close relationship between such regeneration and the "charge" of the tissue. Fritz-Albert Popp saw that there is a "light" in the body responsible for photo-repair of cells and that cancerous compounds block this light and scramble its frequency so that photo-repair can't take place.[1] He found that living organisms must maintain a delicate equilibrium of electro-magnetic "light," and that cancer patients had lost the rhythmic and coherent pulsating of that field of energy. As Lynne McTaggart puts it, "The lines of internal communication were scrambled. They had lost their connection with the world. In effect, their light was going out."[2] As native peoples have generally known, illness should be thought of in terms of isolation, a lack of connection with The Field and the community it supports. This has been shown, to some extent, to be the case also with AIDS and heart disease patients.[3]

Western science is finally connecting with ancient wisdom with regard to the issue of healing. Malidoma Patrice Somé puts it this way: "In an indigenous view of illness, the disease is always linked to a breakage in relationship. Some connection is loose or completely absent or has been severed. What the villager sees in the physical disease is simply the aftermath of something that has happened on the level of energy or relationship. The illness is a physical manifestation of a spiritual decay."[4]

Spiritual decay is what lies at the root of the human

assaults on the natural world. "Seen in this way, nature, the dwelling place of the ancestral spirits, is a vast field of grief. I say this because every harmful thing done to the earth is registered in nature. Nature is the place where the real work of healing takes place slowly and gradually. This is because nature cannot ignore the wounds that humans inflict on one another and on her."[5]

Healing, whether of the individual, of a community, or of the entire earth-community, requires connection, and no individual healing can be complete of itself. We must take seriously the ancient wisdom that healing occurs in the context of human community and of nature as a whole; therefore, an important part of our healing is to learn and to share our human story as part of the story of the earth and of the universe. Such a cosmological grounding provides the encouragement we need when we engage in work that helps heal the earth.

The Universe Story, by Thomas Berry and Brian Swimme, is a poetic and comprehensive narrative of the history of the universe. That telling of the story is, of course, subject to revision according to new knowledge, but the book shows, in a manner never known before, how humans have created what amounts to a contemporary sacred story, the epic of evolution that tells us how the universe came to be, and the sequence of its transformations through billions of years, including the formation of our solar system, and how the earth took shape and brought us into existence. This is our sacred story, our way of making sense of the mystery of our being and of all Being. And, as we saw in Part IV, it is a story, not of some random process, but of *creativity*: of spontaneity and diversity, mutuality and communion.

Like the universe itself, our story about it is a process of development; it changes for us every time we learn something more about the universe's origin and history and manner of functioning. It is especially important that young people become familiar with the earth's origins and development as an integrated life form, its ways of self-preservation and how it nurtures us. Only then are they able to appreciate its gifts and learn how responsibly to help heal its wounded-ness.

In his *Myths to Live By*, Joseph Campbell highlighted the loneliness of the mentally ill person who lacks the reference guides provided by mythology—specifically, the ubiquitous "heroic journey," to be encountered in so much of the world's religious and creative mythology. Much mental illness—and our modern manner of dealing with it—catches people in the trap of trying to avoid suffering at all costs; whereas, the myths all tell us that, unfair as it may seem, there is no true healing of emotional pain without a certain sort of suffering. The myths of the heroic journey reassure us that the suffering can be well worth it: that, if the road to heaven goes through hell, it does lead to heaven. There *can* be room for happiness for those who are willing to take that road.

Two examples of earth-healing, not yet considered in this book, are the struggle against bio-piracy and the work being done to protect the ethnosphere. The Indian physicist Vandana Shiva has helped to clarify the role of modern corporations in the continuation of the colonization of vulnerable peoples and lands through economic treaties, patents and intellectual property rights. Five hundred years after Columbus, she writes, "The Papal Bull has been replaced by the General Agreement on Tariffs and Trade (GATT) treaty. The principle of effective occupation by Christian princes has been replaced by effective occupation by the trans-national corporations supported by modern-day rulers. The 'vacancy' of targeted lands has been replaced by the vacancy of targeted life forms and species manipulated by the new biotechnologies. The duty to incorporate savages into Christianity has been replaced by the duty to incorporate local and national economies into the global marketplace, and to incorporate non-Western systems of knowledge in the reductionism of commercialized Western science and technology . . . Through patents and genetic engineering, new colonies are being carved out. The land, the forests, the rivers, the oceans, and the atmosphere have all been colonized, eroded, and polluted. Capital now has to look for new colonies to invade and exploit for its further accumulation. These new colonies are, in my view, the interior spaces of the bodies of women, plants, and animals. Resistance to biopiracy is a resistance to the ultimate colonization of life itself—of the future of evolution as well as the future of non-Western traditions of relating to and knowing nature. It is a struggle to protect the freedom of diverse species to evolve. It is a struggle to conserve both cultural and biological diversity."[6]

Healing nature must involve us in joining in that resistance: in questioning the right of corporations to control which seeds farmers can plant, along with the chemical fertilizers they must agree to use, in reversing the trend toward forcing whole areas into giving up agricultural diversification for single crops whose sale depends on market forces over which the farmers have no control.

Healing nature must also include doing whatever is possible at this late date to protect what remains of the "ethnosphere," our amazingly rich cultural heritage as a species—for we too are a part of nature. Whole human cultures are disappearing at an almost unbelievable rate. The anthropologist, Wade Davis, reminds us that every two weeks an elder carries a language to the grave. Of the six thousand languages still spoken, half of them are not being taught to children. "It is not change that threatens the ethnosphere; it is power. Dynamic living cultures are being destroyed because of political and economic decisions made by outside entities."[7]

The universe story teaches the values of differentiation and community. Wade Davis applies these values to our predicament: "No single worldview, let alone one with such a shallow history, holds all the keys to our survival as a species . . . These other cultures, so alive and so magical, are not failed attempts at modernity; they are vibrant facets of the diamond of human existence . . . Together the cultures of the world make up an intellectual and spiritual web of life, an ethnosphere that envelops and insulates the planet. It is as vital to our collective well-being as is the biosphere upon which all life depends."

Confronting biopiracy and destruction of the ethnosphere are but two of many ways in which natural healing can take place, as long as there remain people with the knowledge and willingness to engage in those efforts. Healing nature must also take the form of stopping the destruction of the forests, overfishing of the lakes and oceans, depletion of the soil, and so on. The list seems endless, and it is hard to remain optimistic; therefore, we must all act as if we shall succeed, before it is too late.

As indicated often in this book, as well as elsewhere, the underlying issue is one of value, which boils down to a question of connection. People who feel connected to nature could never treat the inhabitants of the land, water and atmosphere in the manner of the corporate polluters and their government accomplices. Rather, the freedom to plunder would give way to the responsibility to heal.

[1] Lynne McTaggart, *The Field*, p. 40.
[2] McTaggart, p. 50f.
[3] McTaggart, p. 194.
[4] Malidome Patrice Somé, *The Healing Wisdom of Africa*. NY: Tarcher/Putnam, 1998, p. 73.
[5] Somé, p. 54.
[6] Vandana Shiva, *Biopiracy: the Plunder of Nature and Knowledge*. Boston: South End Press, 1997. Shiva is " . . . one of India's leading physicists, a leading thinker who has eloquently blended her views on the environment, agriculture, spirituality, and women's rights into a powerful philosophy."—*Utne Reader*.
[7] Wade Davis, "Saving the Ethnosphere," *Boston Globe*, 4/28/02.

Chapter Four

A World For Worship

A religion relevant for our time will need to frame worship in terms of our connection with the real world.

"It is not easy to live in that continuous awareness of things which alone is true living." ~*Joseph Wood Krutch*

"At the center of the Universe dwells Wakan Tanka, and this center is really everywhere; it is within each of us." ~*Black Elk*

"Everything has its song," say the Kwakiutls; "Every person, every animal, and everything has its song and its story." ~*Natalie Curtus,* **The Indians' Book**

"We gather again in worship, concern and celebration. We unite to care for one another, to live our lives with purpose, to be in harmony with the earth. In this community of fellowship we look for wisdom, compassion and strength to follow the rhythm of life's mystery and join in its dance. Formed each moment by the way we live, we welcome life's challenges together." ~*DeKalb, Illinois, Unitarian Universalist Fellowship*

An authority on the world's religions, Huston Smith, received a letter from a man whose son had discontinued his religious studies major at Harvard because "... it was teaching him everything about religion except why anyone would ever believe it."[1] This sort of thing becomes alarming when we consider that no founding city of a civilization has been discovered that does not have a sacred center, some structure that signifies some sort of religious belief.

Our cities seem to be the exceptions. As Joseph Campbell used to say, you can tell a lot about the values held most dear to a community by looking for its tallest building. The cathedrals are now towered over by the houses of financial institutions, which apparently represent the most closely held values of our society. But who would dare to say that those buildings are symbols of anything sacred? Where do we go, in such a society as ours, for a sense of the sacred?

Many now go inward, as some have always done in the religious traditions. A neurologist invites Buddhists and Franciscan nuns to meditate and pray in a secluded room. "At the peak of their devotions, he injects a tracer that travels to the brain and can reveal its activity at the moment of transcendence. A pattern has emerged." The neurologist says there is a small region near the back of the brain that constantly calculates a person's spatial orientation, the sense of where one's body ends, and the world begins. During intense prayer or meditation this region ceases activity, which "... creates a blurring of the self-other relationship ... If they go far enough, they have a complete dissolving of the self, a sense of union, a sense of infinite spacelessness."[2]

The search for a shared physical element in the wide diversity of religious experience has engaged the efforts of scientists at the Harvard University Center for the Study of World Religions. Another well-known researcher is Herbert Benson, president of the Mind/Body Medical Institute and author of *The Relaxation Response*, also affiliated with Harvard. These researchers are looking for a common "biological core" in the world's many varieties of worship as evidence that humans are, in some sense, inherently spiritual beings. A team of researchers at the University of California at San Diego studied patients who suffer from epilepsy and who experience deep religious feelings during the attacks. They found that the seizures strengthened a part of the brain that responds to religious words.

Some will say that such research is evidence that God is a product of the brain; others, that it shows that the brain responds to a higher power. How are we to think about such a question when, for the last hundred years, most influential Western thinkers have believed more in the periodic table of chemical elements than anything in the Bible?

Modern science depends upon controlled experiments. The results of those experiments are considered decisive as long as they can be repeated. But, as Huston Smith pointed out, we can control only what is inferior to us, in the sense of possessing intelligence and the power to influence events. Superior beings, if they exist, must be able to dance circles around us. They know more than we do and will treat our experiments as they please.

This means that we are trying to live fulfilled lives in a

world presumed to be empty of anything superior to us, which makes it an incomplete world according to most, if not all, of the world's religions— and, indeed, many scientists, who recognize that superior beings probably exist somewhere in the universe. Unless you are convinced that humans have made contact with such beings, we are in agreement that a religion relevant for our times will need to frame worship in terms of our respectful connection with the real, natural world, and also of an appreciation of the universe as the primary sacred reality.

A Hopi chief ". . . prays that all the people may have health and long life and be happy and good in their hearts. And Hopis are not the only people he prays for. He prays for everybody in the whole world—everybody. And not people alone; Lololomai prays for all the animals. And not animals alone; Lololomai prays for all the plants. He prays for everything that has life."[3] This is the attitude that should lie at the base of our prayers or meditations—our "language of the heart." This language is always inadequate because it attempts to address what is least known, and yet most deeply felt.

The Rev. Dr. A. Powell Davies, Minister of All Souls Church, Unitarian, in Washington, D.C., from 1944 until his death in 1957, offered this as his benediction for the worship service: "May the little that we know be enough to guide us, while we seek the truth that no one knows, and no one lives without." This is a truth that we may not understand very well but that we may still feel in our aliveness and hear in the tone of our voices.

In the years following the First World War, the Rev. Dr. Norbert Capek, who had been head of all the Baptist churches in Bohemia, embraced more liberal religious convictions and became the leader of the Unitarian movement in Czechoslovakia. (Dr. Capek was ordained into the Unitarian ministry in the Unitarian Church in Orange, New Jersey, where I was minister during the 1970s.) Many of the Czech Unitarians had grown up in other religious communities and expressed a need for ceremonies more suited to their newfound faith. Dr. Capek responded by writing new hymns and devising new rituals, one of the most successful being the Flower Communion service. The various versions of that service, now practiced in most of the Unitarian Universalist churches in North America, reflect a keen sense of connection with nature, as flowers are shared, and freedom, friendship, and the glories of diversity are celebrated.

We read many books about worship and prayer and come away confused by the great range of human religious thought and practice. Searching for a common theme, we find that people usually either hope for some specific result, such as healing, or are simply trying to get in tune with "the powers that be." The motives are various. An often-quoted prayer that illustrates a genuinely pious position is that of the Sufi saint, Rabi'a: "O God! If I worship Thee in fear of Hell, burn me in Hell; and if I worship Thee in hope of Paradise, exclude me from Paradise; but if I worship Thee for Thine own sake, withhold not Thine everlasting beauty!"

How is it, for us to worship God for God's own sake? It is to show respect for the beauty of nature and ourselves as a part of it. Neither fear nor hope, but gratitude is the proper attitude to have, as we come to realize what a miracle it is that we exist at all!—that anything exists at all—and that we live within a nourishing earth community that provides for our needs as long as we show the proper respect.

A Unitarian Universalist unison benediction includes these words: "Respect the earth and all creatures, for they are alive like you." (A version of the entire benediction, first composed by the Rev. Gary Kowalski, may be found in *Singing the Living Tradition*, the Unitarian Universalist hymnbook.)

It is my hope that the words of this book may be of help to those who are trying to develop such a respectful attitude.

[1] Huston Smith, Foreword to *Essays on World Religion*. NY: Paragon House, 1992.
[2] Gareth Cook, "Plumbing the mystery of prayer with the instruments of science." *Boston Globe*, 5/3/01.
[3] Natalie Curtis, *The Indians' Book*. NY: Bonanza Books, 1987, p. 494.

Afterword

As my first edition neared completion, I tuned into public radio in time to hear someone from Ghana say: "What we have is the universe's gift to us. What we become is our gift to the Universe." The universe's values of differentiation, subjectivity and communion give us the freedom to become individuals who may feel responsible enough to give of ourselves for the betterment of the community. We live at a time of promise, but time is running out. In view of the depressing degradations that armored and unconnected people continue to perpetrate, how may we express our gratitude for all that the Universe has given us? What might we give back in return?

We might give our time, talent and treasure to organizations working to deal adequately with the climate crises. We might get more involved, through our religious, political, and social organizations. We might become voices for the forests and oceans, and the animals and plants that live therein.

In 1776, Thomas Paine said, "A long habit of not thinking a thing wrong gives it the superficial appearance of being right." Now we know that much of what people thought right is wrong. We still have the opportunity to reaffirm the intuitive loyalty to life and solidarity of human nature, lift ourselves out of the illusion of isolation, and take ourselves back to reality.

If reading this book helps even one individual with the process of de-armoring and re-connecting, and if it encourages someone who was searching for a philosophical foundation for a religion that respects the natural world, it will have been worth the effort.

I close with this Native American blessing:

> *The life cycle of the creation is endless.*
> *We watch the seasons come and go: life into life, forever.*
> *The child becomes a parent, who then becomes our respected elder.*
> *Life is so sacred!*
> *It is good to be a part of all this.*

Epilogue
to Second Edition

Natural Religion at a Time of Climate Crises

I delivered this sermon at the First Unitarian Universalist Society of Exeter, New Hampshire, on April 28, 2019. Just before my sermon, our church's Minister, the Rev. Kendra Ford, read the poem, "Mountain Ash without Cedar Waxwings," by Robert Pack, who grieves the loss of things we believed to be permanent - the woods, the ocean, the air, and he closes with the question:

Is it too late for me to say,
    for better or for worse,
    I feel as empty as my mountain ash -
    without the cedar waxwings here,
    I feel the loss,
    as wide as our universe,
    of everything that I hold dear?

Some years ago, my wife, Sylvia, and I were canoeing across the lake from our camp in Northwestern Maine when we saw and heard a flock of cedar waxwings on a tree on an island near the shore. It was such a beautiful sight and sound! We still remember it well, even though we have not had that experience since that one time – because their winter home has been destroyed, to make way for soy plantations and cattle farms.

How can we not feel the loss of what we hold dear? How can we fail to grieve the loss of what we have learned to love?

If, as some of us have, you have come to think of the earth as a living organism, then you must realize that planet earth is hurting, is suffering. We have a lot to grieve these days, as ice melts at and near both Northern and Southern poles, and the sea level rises at a much faster rate than was expected, as more than half of the arctic ice is gone, and sea water is more acidic, and temperatures are routinely reaching levels never before recorded.

What has natural religion to do with our hurting earth? A lot! "Religion" comes from the Latin, "religio," meaning to bind together. Everyone whose life is bound together by some sort of coherent way of thinking and acting is religious in that sense. And so the question is whether our religion binds us together in a way that is true to reality – and especially whether we are respectful of the world, as the Unitarian Universalist seventh principle emphasizes: "respect for the interdependent web of all existence of which we are a part" – and, as does the line in the Benediction: "Respect the earth and its creatures, for they are alive like you."

[Rev. Kendra Ford then read another poem: "Control", by May Sarton, concerning the taming of a tiger and the loneliness that mistreating a magnificent but helpless animal may engender with any sensitive person.]

How lonely does that poem make you feel? How lonely do you feel when confronted with the disappearance of songbirds due to rainforest removal or the torture or murder of big game animals by cruel humans?

Some songbirds spend the winter in Brazil. Until recently, that nation was a leader in environmental protection, including reducing deforestation by over 70%. Now, with President Bolsonaro in control, agribusiness, the arms industry and the religious right are in charge – the three Bs: beef, bullets and Bible. Brazil now has the world's highest level of violence against LGBTQ people. Deforestation is again surging. When Bolsonaro visited the US president in Washington he wore a cap with the imprint "Make Brazil Great Again."

Back in the good old U.S. of A., we might ask how it is that our country has done so little to call the fossil-fuel industry to account – an industry that, like the tobacco industry, is known to have lied to the public for a long time concerning the harm of its products, and their production. I agree with Bill McKibben, professor at Middlebury College in Vermont and co-founder of 350.org, that some of our nation's failure to face up to this threat to our well-being and that of the whole earth community is due to the influence of the novelist, Ayn Rand, a promoter of selfishness and unbridled capitalism. That view is upheld by many prominent politicians and other influential people, including the current Vice President, the Secretary of State and the President, who has called "The Fountainhead" his favorite book.

Promoters of Rand's "'philosophy' of objectivism" have included the influential Koch brothers, who have funded many anti-environmental efforts. The irony is, whereas Rand's defenders promote "objectivism" as a sort of scientific objectivity, it really amounts to thinking of others and treating others as objects – that sort of objectivism that is based on contempt, the opposite of empathy. Another Rand disciple, the governor of Wisconsin, prohibited state officials from even mentioning climate change. And the current Administration in Washington has seen to it that the growth of residential solar installations has come to a halt, one of a great many anti-environmental accomplishments.

As a nation, we are on a path to self-destruction, even as solar panels and wind turbines are now among the least expensive ways to produce energy, and storage batteries are cheaper and more effective than ever. A massive program to convert to renewables as envisioned by the Green New Deal is both possible and affordable. All that stands in the way is the power of the fossil-fuel industry, their bought politicians and a duped citizenry. What's changing, as well as the climate, is the rise of a citizen's movement, especially among youth, working to address these issues. I am happy to acknowledge that we are a part of that movement.

But one of the things that confronts us is the fact that most people in our country who think of themselves as "religious" are opposed to natural religion. They are more interested in escaping the real world in favor of their individual salvation. Even so, we may be thankful that many of the younger people who are awakening to the perils we face are not of that persuasion. They would resonate with natural religion, if they don't already, if it were voiced to them in plain language that they can understand – language that conveys both the grief that is a consequence of the of loss of contact with nature and of the love that such contact can engender.

Natural religion affirms what we know by instinct: that we live in a world that is full of feeling, that there is no such thing as a thought without a feeling underneath it, that *feeling* is first in the world at large, and that true morality, including the Golden Rule found in all religions worthy of mention is based in empathy, in sympathetic resonance with another living being, whether human or other animal, or even a plant. Without the ability to feel such sympathy, we are literally lost. That is the essence of natural religion.

As I read Charles Eisenstein's two books that some of you have been reading and discussing – *The More Beautiful World Our Hearts know is Possible* and *Climate A New Story*, I have been pleased to see how much his writing resonates with natural religion, how the themes of wounded-ness due to separation, objectification, and the perverse need to dominate and control. He presents the interconnectedness of all parts of the real world, and in his own words, affirms what John Muir said, "When one tugs at a single thing in nature, he finds it attached to the rest of the world."

Perhaps you've heard this data regarding the human despoiling of planet earth. We learn of whales and sea turtles with 20 to more than 80 pounds of plastic in their stomachs as no more than 9% of plastic waste is being recycled, the rest winding up in landfills and eventually the ocean. We read of huge swaths of the ocean amounting to garbage dumps. The Great Pacific Garbage Patch between Hawaii and California spans an area twice the size of Texas. Every minute an amount of trash, much of it plastic, equal to the contents of a dump truck, enters the ocean. One analysis predicts that by 2050 the plastic in the ocean will outweigh the fish. Dozens of companies, including Dow, Exxon Mobil, Chevron, and Formosa Plastics Corporation formed an "Alliance to End Plastic Waste" pledging one billion dollars to fund recycling and cleanup. That sounds good. But those same companies are also investing $65 billion to expand plastics production in the U.S. and more than 333 new petrochemical projects are underway, including the largest facility of its kind on the Gulf Coast, the result of an agreement by the U.S. president and Saudi Arabia. Exxon alone plans to spend $30 billion on its "Growing the Gulf" venture. The new facilities will require a lot of water in an area already prone to drought and vulnerability to hurricanes. A lot of this is thanks to the fracking revolution that has dramatically lowered the cost of producing plastic, making plastic an important source of profit for Big Oil and providing another reason to drill in the face of climate change.

Those are but a few examples of the results of Big Oil companies contradicting their own scientists concerning climate change and conducting a deliberately deceptive, largely successful PR campaign to convince the public of the harmlessness of their work. Now that more people, including some state governments, have caught on, the companies are trying to convince us that they are genuinely concerned and working to help develop clean energy. That's much too little and too late.

Charles Eisenstein tells us of the importance of grounding environmentalism in something other than data, treated objectively; namely, real emotional contact – in other words – love. The Unitarian, Charles Darwin, devoted a lot of his time to the study of earthworms, not just out of casual interest, but because he was learning what was lovable about them. He came to realize that you cannot love what or whom you don't know AND that, once you really know someone, you will find there something to love – maybe a lot to love.

Eisenstein helps us understand how climate instability/derangement mirrors our own derangement. That insight is nothing new to indigenous people who have always paid close attention to their feeling contact with the other life-beings. Eisenstein wants us to reassert something that has been considered downright sinful in many religions: a sort of animism that enables us to be open to the mind and feeling of nature – so that we may be able to ask, "What does the earth want?" He urges us to pay the close attention that requires us to focus on the specifics: what does this tree want? . . . That forest, this river or stream, this animal, that field of grass and flowers?

What most needs our attention? Ironically, it turns out to be something that gives us the feeling of being alive, of being a living participant in a web of life where every part is connected to every single other part and where, therefore, whatever happens to one part has a real effect on all the rest. No separation.

One of Eisenstein's main points involves his understanding of the problem of reductionism that is all too common in science, whereby, people are inclined to think that "this one thing" matters more than all the rest. So we search for that one thing. These days, for many, it is global warming. Well, global warming certainly does matter. And, yes, it matters to recognize that burning fossil-fuels is a major contributor to global warming, and we need to cut that out sooner rather than later. But if we insist that continuing to burn coal and oil and gas matters so much that we neglect the destruction of forests and grasslands and estuaries and keystone animals and plants, and sources of clean water drying up or being contaminated, then we fail to understand the consequences for global warming, for example, of destroying forests and grasslands and estuaries and polluting the waters. It **all** matters, a lot.

I say this in order to assure you, at a time when many of us feel overwhelmed with all the choices we must make – to the point where we may feel like giving up in despair – that, rather than get all tied up in the search for the one right thing to do, it is better to consult one's own feelings and look for the connection between what one's heart urges and what presents itself as a worthwhile project. Our suffering earth wants a lot! You can see it everywhere you look. So rest assured: you don't have to "get it just right" to make a beneficial impact.

Earth is Creation's gift to us; what do you have to give back? That's worth some thought. Or you may already be clear about that. It need not be only one thing. You may choose to give money to an environmental group who works to protect forests and the ocean and endangered species and also find something near at hand where you can take a hands on approach – planting trees, cleaning up a polluted site, taking care of a suffering animal, joining the campaign to pressure Nestle and others to stop using single-use plastic packaging. Remember: it's all connected, and you may never know the extent of the impact your good piece of work might have. Think of the impact of one Swedish teenager who decided to protest government inaction on global warming and, as I write this, is in New York to meet with United Nations representatives on behalf of the world's young people.

What or who do you love? How well do you know your love? What does that person or animal or tree or stream want or need? Let it speak to you. Whether it is promoting land regeneration or opposing a fracked methane pipeline, finding ways to reduce if not eliminate the use of plastic bags and other containers, to help protect keystone species such as beavers, wolves, bats and bees, – and turn away from poisonous pesticides such as Roundup and insecticides that are killing off whole populations of beneficial insects, getting rid of poisonous pollutants in your house or apartment – there is no end of things you can do if you put your mind and heart to it.

My emphasis here is on the religious. It's about wounded-ness, ours and the earth's, and on separation and the curse of objectification and on the perniciousness of control and lack of caring. It's about empathy. It's about seeing the sacredness of life in all its forms, even those that can do us harm. It's about re-connecting with the real world in ways that help with earth's healing. Our own healing goes with it.

The most quoted verse of the Bible, John 3:16, begins by saying, "For God so loved the world." As Wendell Berry pointed out, that's not God's love for Heaven or for the world as it might be, but for the world as it *is*. That clearly implies the lovability of the world. Well, if God loves the world – if the world is truly lovable – then human destruction of the world is not just bad stewardship; it amounts to a monstrous blasphemy against the Creator. It is flinging God's gift into her face, as of no worth beyond that which we may assign to it, as if it all exists solely for our benefit. For those who may be interested in more of what the Bible teaches, it should be important to understand that we have there no entitlement to destroy or hold in contempt anything on earth or in the heavens or in the waters. We have a right to use the gifts of nature, but not to ruin or waste them. We can use what we need, but no more, which is why the Bible forbids usury and great accumulations of property.

What's more, the Jewish prophets, including of course, Jesus, taught that a sense of the holiness of life is not compatible with an exploitive economy. It is not possible to know that life is holy if you are content to live from economic practices that daily destroy life and diminish its possibility. The prophet Isaiah was very direct in asking: "What do you mean by crushing my people, by grinding the face of the poor?"

It is ironic indeed that "the religion of the Bible" has been perverted by some people into a religion of people who worship money and power over others, a religion that stands silently by while a predatory economy ravages the world and plunders whole human communities. As part of the normal practice of power, the modern Caesar prepares to destroy the world, by spending two trillion dollars to upgrade our nuclear war fighting capacity, thereby, perpetuating another nuclear arms race. Former U.S. Defense Secretary William Perry calls that "insane." Well, that's what it is: insane.

How we live in this world, how we work, how we think of ourselves and others, how we think and feel about the earth and its creatures – these are questions of the gravest religious significance. When, on the other hand, we understand that we are living parts of the earth organism, acting our parts among other creatures, all made of the same earth, then our acts have significance, and we may become soulful artists of living.

Joseph Campbell wrote regarding a mythology for our time that he called "no more horizons," meaning that as we explore both inner and outer worlds there is no end to what we may discover. I hope that will include more realization of our capacity for love, empathy and the feeling of interconnectedness with all life that propels us to works of both self-healing and earth-healing.

In order to facilitate such healing we must first learn how to stop numbing ourselves, by drugs and distracting entertainments and communication devices. We might even re-visit the concept of the kingdom of God as proclaimed by Jesus whose parable of the mustard plant (a wild, invasive plant) had God's reign on earth as subversive of the empire of his day. There's also the Gospel of Thomas' teaching that God's kingdom is "spread out over all the earth; but men do not see it." Maybe if we learn to look more through the eyes of children, and, yes, of women, and certainly of indigenous people, we will see more of it.

In the words of an elder of the Kogi tribe of the Columbian Sierra Nevada concerning the vegetation and waters that humans are destroying and polluting, "If you knew she could feel, you would stop."

Natural religion is a religious philosophy that is rooted in a sense of the intrinsic value of nature, of the sacredness of the interdependent web of life, and of love of the real world, where, if we open ourselves, we may, as the song "Great Trees" has it, ". . . be pleased to walk in radiance amazed" as the "light comes down to earth" and it is "praised."

Love and loss go together, like it or not. To feel that love in its fullness, we must feel the loss of what we hold dear. Only then can the love stay rooted in us and grow.

www.ingramcontent.com/pod-product-compliance
Lightning Source LLC
Chambersburg PA
CBHW020847090426
42736CB00008B/268